EXMOOR VILLAGE

EXMOOR VILLAGE

*Celebrating the Enduring Landscape of Exmoor
and its People Over Fifty Years*

Based on the book *Exmoor Village*
with additional text and photographs
by Hilary Binding and Brian Pearce

EXMOOR
BOOKS

This edition first published in Great Britain in 2004
based on the original work *Exmoor Village* by W.J. Turner, photographs by John Hinde,
© 1947, 2004 Mass Observation Archive Trustees, University of Sussex.

New text in this edition © 2004 Brian Pearce and Hilary Binding,
Copyright © 2004 Exmoor Books and Exmoor National Park Authority.
Copyright on individual photographs in the new edition is acknowledged.

British Library Cataloguing-in-Publication Data
A CIP record for this title is available from the British Library

ISBN 0 86183 486 0

EXMOOR BOOKS
Dulverton, Somerset

*Exmoor Books is a partnership between
The Exmoor Press and The Exmoor National Park Authority*

Trade Sales Enquiries:
Halsgrove House
Lower Moor Way
Tiverton EX16 6SS
Tel: 01884 243242
Fax: 01884 243325
email: sales@halsgrove.com
website: www.halsgrove.com

Printed and bound in Great Britain by CPI Bath

FOREWORD

by Steven Pugsley
Chairman of the Exmoor National Park Authority

THE fiftieth anniversary of any organisation is a proper occasion for reflection and celebration. As Exmoor National Park marks its Golden Jubilee it can regard with some pride its success in the longer term in conserving and enhancing the landscape, flora and fauna of this remarkably precious area. This is not an easy task and perhaps the Park's greatest triumph has been in mediating between the demands of the State (at least, today) for protection of scenery, and the needs of the local population.

For landscape is neither inert nor constant: however wild Exmoor may appear, much of what we value about it has been influenced or indeed achieved by man, and continuing intervention is needed to maintain what most people want to see. One of the more heartening developments in thinking about our protected landscapes is the increasing concern for the people that live in them, have shaped them through history and whose active participation is needed to keep them special.

The work of Mass Observation in wartime Luccombe captured an Exmoor community just as its way of life, essentially unchanged for centuries, was coming to an end. The war might not have caused the huge changes in mobility, technology and agriculture it experienced, but it undoubtedly accelerated them. Aspirations and expectations changed with them. Meanwhile, outside pressures on the Exmoor economy, its infrastructure and housing in succeeding decades, have only served to underline the fragility of its communities (and it is yet to be seen whether ongoing reform of agricultural support will deliver a spur or a body blow).

The National Park cannot stop change. But it can soften its effects and help to keep people at the heart of the Exmoor landscape. As Brian Pearce explains later in this book, it has aided land-based business with grants, it has supported tourism and encouraged appropriate industries in the same way. It has persuaded tourists to support local services and buy local produce. Through its own work as an employer it pumps money into the local economy. Through development control it ensures that most new houses built in the Park are affordable and for local people.

As the Exmoor National Park now looks towards its centenary, it can anticipate with some justice that Mass Observation visiting our Exmoor Village in 2040 would find that the National Park had made a positive difference to the lives and livelihood of its inhabitants. If by doing so it had kept the people who know and understand and love the place, living and working in the landscape, then it would have done much to achieve the purposes for which it was created in the first place.

ACKNOWLEDGEMENTS

Hilary Binding and Brian Pearce would like to thank everyone who has provided them with information and illustrations for this book. Besides those credited in the text they would like to thank especially the staff at Dulverton Heritage Centre for access to the Exmoor Photographic Archive, Michael Deering, who prepared the Archive, and Allerford Museum for access to their collections. We would also like to thank Dr Robert Dunning, Birdie Johnson and the Exmoor Archive, and also the National Trust and Somerset Record Office. We have struggled to find the copyright holders for some of the photographs and if we have missed you please forgive us and let us know who you are!

The publishers record their thanks to the Mass Observation Archive Trustees at the University of Sussex, particularly Dorothy Sheridan, who kindly gave permission to use material from the original *Exmoor Village*.

PREFACE

The origins of the original book *Exmoor Village*, which is at the heart of the present volume lie with the organisation Mass-Observation. Mass-Observation was founded in 1937 by Tom Harrisson, an anthropologist, and Charles Madge, a writer and poet. Its purpose was to create 'an anthropology of ourselves', an account of the everyday life of modern Britain through observing and recording the doings, thoughts and feelings of its people, particularly ordinary people. Those who carried out the work were to be 'the people' themselves, a 'panel' of volunteer observers who would carry on their work alongside their everyday lives and within their own communities. M-O made use of the standard techniques of the still very new market research, like interviews and door-to-door questionnaires. It centred on the 'observation' of everyday life and the 'directive'. In the former case observers were literally that. They watched people and listened to their conversations and they followed them in streets noting how they behaved – hardly behaviour acceptable today even in the interests of scientific research! The directives were different. These asked the observer to focus on particular ideas of issues via their own feelings, local knowledge and conversation with those around them.

Through the late 1930s M-O attracted a good deal of often sensational newspaper coverage, particularly when they touched on a taboo subject such as sexual behaviour, or subject of public curiosity like drinking, gambling or astrology. It was however during the Second World War that their most interesting and, to the historian at least, most valuable material was produced. Although much of the pre-war 'observation' was abandoned, for obvious reasons, it was replaced by observers keeping diaries. Here are recorded the everyday anxieties, problems and triumphs of ordinary people at war.

M-O only just survived the war. Madge left the organisation, Harrisson lost interest and the numbers of volunteer 'observers' declined and in 1950 the organisation was wound up, although its name continued to be used by a public opinion company M-O (UK) Ltd. However when Harrisson became founding Professor of Anthropology at the University of Sussex he brought with him the organisation's archive, which is now housed in the University Library.

In 1981 Dorothy Sheridan, the Archivist restarted the project on a new but similar basis. As in the 1930s, a volunteer panel was recruited who reply to directives and keep diaries but do not follow people around the streets or eavesdrop! The material produced by M-O is unique in these islands, if not the world, and has been widely used by researchers, the media, and students at Sussex. Much of this work has been about urban areas but, even in its earliest work, there are some representatives of rural communities, while the wartime diaries and directives contain more. This material was widely used in my book *The Death of Rural England. A social history of the countryside since 1900* published in 2003.

The study of Luccombe was however their only entirely rural project. The study was commissioned, as the original introduction says, as part of an intended series on 'people and their ways of life' and bears the name of W.J.Turner, a poet and country writer, as its author. In fact, as the material held at Sussex shows, much of the material was written by two M-O workers Desinee Ivey and Nina Masel. Turner, according to one woman in Luccombe, only came to the village once! This however has proved an advantage, in my view at least, since the writing is mostly free of the sentimental romanticising that destroys so much writing about rural communities.

The book, when originally published, received mixed reviews and, according to M-O's follow-up, produced a similar reaction in the village. Some felt 'shock' and 'indignation' especially at things like the description of their possessions as 'cheap'. Others viewed it more positively, especially those who relied at least in part on summer visitors for part or all of their income, who hoped it would attract 'a lot of visitors'. By the 1950s the book had sunk without trace outside Luccombe, and even the series on the village shown on HTV in 1988 and presented by Daniel Farson made little impact. Yet the book remains extremely important. It is also unusual in that it was written from inside and very much through the voices of the villagers, even if those voices were mediated through M-O. For that reason alone its reprint is extremely welcome to those who study the rural areas. This value is hugely increased by the new material. I can only hope that the new *Exmoor Village* will not vanish in the way the old one did.

For those who would like to know a bit more about M-O and the countryside the journal *Rural History. Economy, Society, Culture*, published two articles in Volume 9 no. 1, in April 1998. One by myself called 'A Country at war: Mass-Observation and Rural England, 1939–45' and one by Jacqueline Sarsby on the photographs in Exmoor Village called 'Exmoor Village Revisited; Mass-Observation and Wartime Colour Photography'. If you are interested in learning more about the current work of M-O contact them by e-mail at www.sussex.ac.uk/library/massobs, or by post at The Mass-Observation Project, The University of Sussex Library, Brighton BN1 9QL.

Alun Howkins
Professor of Social History
University of Sussex.

CONTENTS

PART ONE

EXMOOR IN THE 1940s

An Introduction to the New Edition

by Hilary Binding

When the Mass-Observation Team visited Luccombe in 1944 Britain was caught up in war and Sir Richard Acland had just given Luccombe, as part of the Holnicote Estate, to the National Trust. In the welter of detail recorded about Luccombe in *Exmoor Village* these important events seem to merit only incidental mention.

During the war a number of Luccombe men and women served in the forces and the names of four who died are recorded on the war memorial in the church. Evacuees were accommodated in the farms and cottages – seven at least attended the village school – and men in reserved occupations served in the Home Guard. Rationing affected everybody although it is true that in the countryside people had the advantage of supplementary vegetables, milk direct from the farm and the occasional rabbit or pheasant for the pot. Petrol was in short supply.

Maybe the parameters of the Team's questions limited what could be asked but the result seems to me to provide only a two-dimensional picture of a village, representative of much of Exmoor, that was on the cusp of change. It seems strange to look at charming photographs of the Luccombe countryside knowing that on some of the surrounding hills military training was taking place.

In this introduction I offer a personal view of Exmoor in the 1940s. There are a number of published sources that give more detail of the war particularly and this account does not claim to be in any way compre-

In the Valley of Luccombe. Picture postcards like this one were sent by visitors to folks at home, often with the message: 'Wish you were here!'

hensive. It may, however, provide, often in the words of people who lived on Exmoor, a flavour of everyday life at the time.

Conserving Exmoor

The idea of conserving the beauty and nature of Exmoor for the enjoyment of the public was not new in 1954 when Exmoor became a National Park. In February 1917, in a letter to *The Times*, it was announced that Sir Charles Thomas Dyke Acland of Holnicote and Killerton in Devon had placed his Exmoor estates under the permanent guardianship of The National Trust.

'The Trust will not become the owner of the lands,' the letter read. Sir Thomas was to grant the lands to the Trust on a 500-year lease and he and his successors would continue to enjoy the rents and profits and all the ordinary rights and powers of an owner except that of developing the estate as a building estate. The Trust obtained control over any powers that might be necessary to preserve the property, so far as possible, in its present beauty and natural condition.

The letter continued: 'The new property will not be a source of income to the Trust. But it will, we hope and believe, be something better than that. We believe that in agreeing to take this new departure, and, for the first time, accept something less than ownership, the Trust is finding a new and useful means of discharging its duty to the nation and that many generations of Englishmen who will visit Exmoor in the future will gratefully remember the name of Sir Thomas Acland, whose forethought and generosity preserved for them one of the most beautiful pieces of wild country to be found in England.'

Just after the outbreak of the Second World War Sir Richard Acland inherited the family estates of Killerton, near Exeter, and Holnicote. He had been elected Liberal MP for North Devon in 1935 but, according to his wife Anne, had been converted to socialism and led his own 'Common Wealth' party during the war, advocating common ownership for moral, and not merely economic, reasons. In 1944 he made a gift of all the land in his possession on the Killerton and Holnicote estates to The National Trust 'partly as a matter of principle and partly in order to preserve them intact for future generations.'

Cicely Cooper, who became headmistress of Allerford School in 1940, recalled in her *Memoirs of Selworthy and West Somerset* the handing over of the Holnicote estate.

'One of the most momentous days in the history of Selworthy or Holnicote Estate was that on which it was transferred from the ownership of Sir Richard Acland to that of the National Trust. The actual transfer of the property took place in the School, where nearly all the parish functions are celebrated.

'The great day came! Armfuls of rhododendrons arrived to decorate the schoolroom, and though it was a time of year when there were few flowers, yet the ladies contrived to make a very fair show. The platform was put up, and all along it were bowls of snowdrops and violets and much greenery. Jasmine brightened the bunches of laurel around walls and bright pink rhododendrons in clusters made it all look very gay. On the platform my chair and desk were draped ready for the celebrities.

'One lives in this part of Holnicote Estate without ever realising that it is part of a large family – a distinct unity – it is so widely scattered. Every tenant on the Estate had been invited to attend the function, and I was amazed when they arrived. One is so used to seeing bus loads of visitors driving through that it does not occur to you that the real Holnicote is rarely seen and never gathered together in these days – though I believe it used to muster at a great Parish Festival in olden days. The tenants foregathered on horses or on foot – not in cars, as one seems to expect.

Piles Mill, Allerford, 1941.

Nags were tied up to the railings, sheep dogs hurtled about the School yard.

'The babel of an unknown tongue only heard on the Exmoor hills filled the air – greetings were called in voices used to the hailing of sheep up aloft, and hounds thumped their excited tails on the School floor. One of these independently minded beasts roved through my window and lapped up a jug of milk in my absence.

'A good feed was spread out in the School, though I fear poor in comparison with the hearty fare these people were used to in the great days of Holnicote. I have heard of sides of bacon, rounds of beef, bowls of cream, kegs of cider, etc., but, of course, we only had sandwiches and cake. But I have seen a great deal of eating done in Allerford School, and none with more hearty goodwill than this feast. Dogs looked hungrily up and helped themselves to an occasional sausage roll.

'It was the most remarkable meeting I have seen at Allerford, because of its atmosphere of gathering of the distant clans. Usually at our assemblies we never saw the hill people. On the platform were Sir Richard and Lady Acland, looking very young, indeed, Sir Richard rather like a schoolboy home for the holidays – or that at least was his manner – and that is how he talked later, not like the able Parliamentarian of whom we read in the papers.

'The Rectors of Selworthy and Luccombe and Sir George Trevelyan, with other representatives of the National Trust, and old Mr. Floyd, of Bossington, were there. There was one notable absence – Mr John Acland, whose health prevented his coming. But he, as Rector's Warden, and the one member of the family who had lived so entirely among us, was sadly missed.

'Sir Richard made a careful, lucid speech in which he set forth simply his reasons for giving up his estate. He might hope to be understood by these people who dwell in this beautiful district, but I think that though the real soil-born natives have a patriotism fierce enough, it is not at all because of the superior beauty of the place but just because it is their home. It is the outsiders who worship the scenery of Holnicote and know it to be of such unique loveliness that Sir Richard, in trying to preserve it intact for ever, was doing an understandable thing. For all I heard the farmers say afterwards was to the effect that they couldn't make head nor tail of "Young Dick". He could "put it over" anyway, and with a wink that implied they scarcely credited his disinterested philanthropy. But, of course, an outsider like myself is not likely to penetrate the real thoughts of the people. I never had a chance to know them well. But I cannot escape the conclusion that they are hardheaded, not prone to generous appreciation, but suspicious always of having the wool pulled over their eyes by someone apparently more astute than they feel themselves to be.

'The biggest laugh was gained by old Mr Floyd of Bossington when he began his reminiscences. The audience roared and clapped, and the dogs barked at the thought that he at least didn't know what he was up there to talk about. The platform guests caught the spirit of the joke and ended by thumping him on the back, so in hearty good spirits we went home not wondering much about the National Trust but thinking about a changed England and whether it were for the best. There was much head wagging!'

Freddie Reeks, Steward on the Holnicote Estate for Sir Richard Acland, had by this time, I believe, gone off to war and on his return as colonel took up the reins as agent for the National Trust. The author of *Exmoor Village* comments that by 1947 the National Trust had done little save 'at Webber's Post set up a collecting box and list of prohibitions. So far there is nothing either inviting or informative in their notices.' Not a very promising start!

Holnicote Estate Staff, Autumn 1948. Many of these men had worked on the Holnicote Estate all their lives. Names supplied by John Court, 1995.
(Left to right:) Fred Blackmore, carpenter; Jack Kingdom, gardener; Keeper Seaward; Reg Tame, carpenter; Bill Ford, labourer; Stan Warren, painter; Mr Glassborough, secretary; Charlie Hooper, labourer; John Court, mason; Jack Gould, mason; Tim Webber, gardener; Stan Thompson, forester; Mr Harrison, head forester; Bill Gould, forester; Tom Hole, labourer; Harold Prescott, driver; Laurie Lad, plumber; George Hughes, lorry driver; Tom Harris, head gardener; Derek Farmer, forester; Evan Keal, carter; Mr Parkhouse, foreman; Arthur Kingdom, thatcher; Bill Tame, forester; Raymond Keal, sawyer.

Courtesy: The National Trust

Wartime

The Second World War affected everyone: rationing, restrictions, voluntary work, uprooting of families, loss. A rural area like Exmoor might escape the horrors of direct nightly bombing but its proximity to the Bristol Channel and the nearby bombing of Bristol and Cardiff meant that planes were continually overhead and there were numerous incidents of planes coming down on the moor. It was, however, the influx of evacuees that made the greatest impression and long before war broke out the people of Exmoor were gearing themselves up to welcome huge numbers of evacuees from the cities into their homes. They began to arrive before war was declared and continued to do so until it was nearly over.

Dulverton, according to the RDC minutes, was in 1940 prepared to accept nearly 1500 evacuees; women and children from London – Dagenham, West Ham and Barking – and from the South Coast. Although some returned to their homes quite soon, others stayed and more arrived at regular intervals over the next few years. Among them were many 'unofficial' evacuees who had made their own way to Exmoor and made their own arrangements for accommodation. A census of evacuees in the Dulverton area made in July 1942 listed 338 unaccompanied children, 188 women with children, 51 adults, 28 teachers and helpers and 46 boys in camps. Among houses requisitioned in the area was Ashwick, which was turned into a hostel for women and children. The Retreat at Dulverton became a sick bay while the Club at Dulverton and the Youth Hostel at Exford were used as clearing houses. Baths were taken at the Parish Rooms at Dulverton.

In the early 1940s there were still schools in most Exmoor villages. Although many pupils had just a few minutes walk to school, those who lived two, three or more miles distant across fields or via lanes made their way sometimes on foot but also on ponies or by bicycle.

Well before the outbreak of war Exmoor schools, remote, parochial and insular, had been warned to expect evacuees. At the start of the Autumn Term in 1939 all schools were closed for ten days to prepare for the advent of evacuees but as the Headmistress at Withiel Florey noted when she opened a week or so later: 'There don't seem to be many about as yet.' That situation soon changed. Unofficial evacuees registered as ordinary pupils in local schools but when the official evacuees with their teachers arrived there were often so many that they had to be taught in alternative accommodation.

On 1 September 1939, just two days before war was declared, 468 children accompanied by 46 teachers and helpers arrived in West Somerset. Pupils at Gainsborough School in Canning Town, West Ham, had been standing by to evacuate for the past year but had only a few hours' warning when they were actually told to go.

The late Roy Chenappa, who helped co-ordinate the evacuation, remembered the journey well. 'I was the only one with a telephone so it was up to me to contact the stationmaster and organise things. There were children from other local schools in West and East Ham who came along too. Nobody knew where their destination would be, although they had an idea they could be going to the Oxford area. My wife soon put us straight. As the children were stomping across the platform at Ealing Broadway a porter called out: "Mind your feet! Mind your heads! Watch it!" and then whispered to my wife that that was where we were going.'

Evacuees with local pupils at Wootton Courtenay School. Roy Chenappa is at the back on the left.

Dorothy and John Ball, Exmoor Photographic Archive

At Williton, 360 children and 34 adults including Gainsborough head-master George Baber ended their journey. The rest of the party went on to Minehead and were welcomed to West Somerset at Alcombe Village Hall. There they were given something to eat and the children were allo-cated foster parents. They were then sent to Wootton Courtenay, Timberscombe, Luccombe and Porlock as well as Alcombe and Minehead. Ten children and one master even went out as far as Oare.

Pupils were not always happy and there were problems in some foster homes. Roy Chenappa remembered one ten-year-old lad who arrived on his doorstep announcing in no uncertain terms that he was going home. When he reminded the boy that he had no money and that London was 200 miles away, the lad simply replied, 'I don't care. I'll walk.'

The teaching staff organised a timetable at St Michael's School in Minehead. Local children were taught in the morning and evacuees had lessons after lunch. One evacuee who wrote to the *West Somerset Free Press* in 1999, Evelyn Bassett (née Everett), remembered how cramped it was at the school and recalls having her domestic science lessons in the railway shed at the station, washing and ironing handkerchiefs! Later Alcombe Village Hall became their school. All over Exmoor halls and meeting rooms were commandeered and turned into teaching accommodation.

In June 1940 pupils from Leytonstone arrived in Withypool and an evacuee school was set up in the WI Hut. The next day there was an 'official' meeting on the Green between local pupils and evacuees where they joined together in PT and Games and ended the day by listening to a story. One can imagine the children circling each other like sheep dogs warily keeping an eye on recalcitrant sheep. A little later in the month 26 more children from West Ham arrived and trestles and forms were brought in from the chapel so that these pupils could be accommodated in the school itself.

Withypool was a school with problems during the 1940s – one pupil remarked that there were seven different head teachers during her time there. This is backed up by the school log book, which records teachers unable to cope with older boys wanting to be at work, difficult caretakers, unreliable supplies of coal for essential school heating (the stove), appalling sanitary arrangements and snow.

Stella Carroll came to Withypool as an unofficial evacuee in 1941 at the age of three. She was found a home with Fred and Madge Blackmore, farmers, who welcomed her and made her feel that she belonged. She was soon enrolled at the village school – just a two-roomed building, the big room for the older children, the small one at the back for the younger ones. Miss Condon was the teacher when Stella arrived and the little girl found her easy going and caring. She soon found friends.

At the time Withypool seemed almost self-sufficient, with everyone growing vegetables and salad stuff. Bread, butter and milk were all home produced and there was plenty of fruit. Nothing was wasted. Even the lambs' tails were cooked, cut off with a sharp knife and made into lamb's tail pie. 'In the evenings I would go round to friends' houses or they would come to us. If it were raining we'd play in the barn or in the sheds across the fields. Sometimes we'd go down to the river Barle, paddle and catch small fish. In good weather we'd go up to the moor and pick worts. There was no fear of traffic or strangers then as we never saw any; the only form of transport was farmers' horses and carts. Sunday was a ritual: church in the morning, chapel in the afternoon and Sunday school after tea. I loved it.'

At Allerford, where the evacuees and local children were taught together, it seems that were real problems at first. Cicely Cooper was appointed to deal with the situation. She describes her first morning: 'I approached the School door confidently to hear an uproar going on in the porch. Violent Cockney abuse was being hurled at some irate teacher, and presently the door flew open and out was thrust by a strong arm clutching the back of the neck a struggling, kicking mass of boyhood, which collapsed on the floor and howled.

'One look at the teacher told me that she was an experienced disciplinarian who would not have resorted to such expulsion except under undue strain … Well, if this pantomime repeated itself I should be lost, I thought. I stayed outside thinking. Normal children only go berserk like animals when badly frightened. What was frightening them? Not the Managers certainly, nor the people of Allerford, nor even this very competent looking teacher, who, I think, had just lost heart and patience for the moment. No! It was the uprooting, shaking away of all familiar contacts and habits, fear of the blitz at home and then being left in charge of a teacher divested of the surroundings and authority of a big London school.'

Evacuees who lived with the Harris family at Pump Cottage, Allerford

Allerford Museum

Miss Cooper's assessment of the relationship between the evacuees and the local children may well have been common to many Exmoor schools. 'I will not say that the evacuees and the natives ever came to love each other,' she wrote. 'My impression is that strangers are resolutely shut out from the West Countryman's understanding. But the two groups learnt to respect each other's individuality, live very congenially and work happily together' although many of the evacuees certainly seized the first possible opportunity to return to London.

In some cases schools more than doubled their intake. At Brompton Regis 37 evacuees joined 26 local pupils while at Timberscombe there were 35 local pupils, 35 official evacuees and five unofficial. Here a double timetable was followed, half the pupils being taught in the morning and half in the afternoon. At tiny Treborough 13 evacuees joined 14 local pupils.

On 26 May 1941 Miss Cook arrived at Withiel Florey School with nine pupils from Bristol. A form had to be borrowed from the nearby farm so that all the 35 pupils had something to sit on. It was decided to run a double timetable: Miss Cook would take all the seniors in the morning (9.30am-1.30pm) while the juniors would be taught by Mrs Jenkins in the afternoon (1.30pm-5.30pm.) Mothers soon complained about the long day, which was then reduced by an hour. In June it was decided to open a room at the farm to accommodate half the school but it took months to get it fit for use and it was not opened until 3 December. The plan was that senior pupils should be taught at the farm although Harold Bale of Burrow Farm, remembering his school days at Withiel Florey, recalls that the evacuees occupied the school building whilst the local children adjourned to the farmhouse. Whatever the circumstances, the room remained in use until 30 July 1943.

At Simonsbath 23 boys and seven girls arrived from Goodall Road School in Leyton with their teacher, Frank Betts. Once they had settled into their new homes, an evacuee school was set up in the old Gospel Hall which was then known as the Meeting House. In 1942 the village school and the evacuee school were amalgamated and the Meeting House used as a second classroom.

Each school had its own procedure to be followed in case of an air raid. Gas masks were, of course, carried to school and home again and the Gas Masks Drill meant that pupils were able to don their masks at a moment's notice. They were also given instructions on what to do if there was an air raid warning. In small villages pupils were expected to run to school or back home depending on which was the nearer while if they were on a two or three-mile trek across the fields to an isolated farm they were warned to put on their gas masks and lie under a hedge. If the alarm was given at Treborough while pupils were in school, they were to don their gas masks, go to a nearby field and lie under a hedge or in the bracken. At Withycombe they were expected to run to the Rectory garden (divine protection?) or to the fields. In other schools pupils simply lay on the floor away from the windows. There were no sirens in the villages to warn of an air raid – instead there was a telephone link. The Civil Defence Wardens in each parish would receive a call from the CD headquarters at Townsend House in Minehead where Colonel Moriarty was in charge. There was also a telephone link with the village policeman, then to be found in most parishes. Ann le Bas of Winsford has no recollection of any children on Exmoor ever having to act on the precautions. Ann's father was Civil Defence Divisional Warden in the Dulverton area while Ann herself was involved in training.

Many evacuees enjoyed their time on Exmoor – letters of thanks were received by Dulverton RDC from the head teachers of schools at Barking and West Ham while the mistress-in-charge of Tenterden children wrote:

The last pupils at Wootton Courtenay school, 1946. Miss Griffin with Bill Lang, David Rawle, Andrew Slade, Pam Carter, Archie Dyer.
Front row: Phyl Barclay (Quick), Chrissie Brooks, Belinda Jury, Albert Slade.

Allerford Museum

'We know that no evacuees anywhere could have been happier than we were.' Some evacuees never left the area while others kept in touch with their hosts and returned in later years to revisit childhood haunts and recall happy days. Once the evacuees had left, several Exmoor schools like that at Wootton Courtenay closed

Very many people in both towns and villages were involved in Fire Defence, the Women's Voluntary Service, the Home Guard, Civil Defence, the Observer Corps and as Air Raid Wardens. But ordinary housewives also worked hard for the war effort 'keeping the home fires burning'. *A Celebratory History of a Village WI* edited by Hilda Parham and Christine Dore in 1990 gives an account of the activities of the Dunster WI during the war. It is typical of many villages across the country.

'In November 1939 sugar for preserving was distributed to members, and the Sugar Club started for jam making and fruit preservation, part of

Porlock WI market, 1944
Sir Robin Dunn (Allerford Museum)

a government scheme set up to enable householders to preserve local fruit crops. In 1940 jam was made and sold for 1s 3d per two pounds at the Yarn Market Stall and in local shops. Dunster jam was of high quality and in 1941 half a ton was made. By 1942 the Government fruit preservation scheme made possible the canning of locally grown pears and other fruit and this went on until at least 1949. By 1945 members had made 2,813lbs of jam to say nothing of all the chutney prepared and fruit canned. The Yarn Market Stall ran throughout the war years, selling vegetables and fruit given by villagers plus jams and canned fruit; the proceeds going to the Red Cross.

Dunster Wool and Comforts Fund was set up in January 1940 – socks and helmets were knitted and camouflage hats made for the army. The fund provided knitted comforts for local men serving in the Forces and in the first year 133 parcels were sent out each containing socks, gloves, writing paper and a cake (all made by WI members). By 1945, 871 parcels had been sent off and many grateful letters received in return.

Early in the war the Dunster Beach Chalets were commandeered as an Army Rest Centre, with a new intake of troops each fortnight. The Vicar of Dunster, the Rev. A. H. Balleine, was keen that a canteen should be provided for the soldiers and the WI agreed to run the canteen and provide the meals. It was open each evening at the Memorial Hall and despite the restrictions of rationing (maybe there was a special allowance) members provided plenty of food; eggs and beans, apple pies, blancmanges, tarts and cakes made by older members while the younger ones waited at table. Up to 19 November 1940 it is reported that 8,596 meals were cooked and 11,598 cups of tea served. One evening 100 eggs were fried!

By 1944 the Red Cross working party was meeting every Friday to make bandages and handkerchiefs and garments for prisoners of war. When, in 1944, a big Fete was held in aid of the Red Cross, the WI made a house to house collection for rationed foods so that it was able to serve 1,400 teas.

The Exmoor Mounties

The LDV – Local Defence Volunteers, soon renamed the Home Guard – were established in May 1940. Exmoor was unique in having a mounted patrol made up of people associated with the Devon and Somerset Staghounds which had established itself very quickly and by August numbered about fifty men. Some were mounted on Exmoor ponies that were sure-footed and knew the terrain. The first CO of the unit was Mr S. L. Hancock, Master of the Devon and Somerset Staghounds, and when he left for army service Bernard Waley Cohen, one of the hunt's joint secretaries, took over. The third CO was Colonel Robert Dundas Alexander of Porlock, a former Master of the Exmoor Foxhounds. In the early days Ernest Bawden, huntsman for 20 years to the D and S, was a section commander. He was to die in a farming accident during the war.

The mounted patrols did duties in fours each night and kept watch from positions near Brightworthy Barrows and the corner of Alscombe Common on the Withypool-Sandyway road amongst others. At first they carried shotguns and buckshot ammunition – not to mention in some places cudgels, knives, homemade coshes and even billhooks – but eventually were issued with rifles.

Colonel Alexander gave up command of the Exmoor Mounties when he became CO of the 1st Somerset (Minehead) Home Guard battalion, whose territory stretched from Exmoor through the West Somerset Vale and into the Quantocks and Brendons. Companies or platoons were based on Minehead, Dunster, Porlock, Exford and Dulverton as well as Williton, Watchet, Stogumber, Bicknoller, Crowcombe and Wiveliscombe. A Brendon Hill platoon was attached to the Wiveliscombe company.

A mounted signalman of the 1st Somerset (Minehead) Battalion Home Guard with his R/T 1944

Mounted patrols like this one covered extensive areas of Exmoor

Besides patrol and guard duties that released the regular army for other tasks, Home Guards were responsible for setting up and manning roadblocks. They had authority – which they often exercised with delighted enthusiasm – to demand to see a person's identity card. They could expect a bit of banter from their own villagers but it was best not to try to be too clever!

Sometimes training was carried out alongside the regular army and the latter did not always come off best. But the greatest rivalry was between Home Guard companies. A favourite Exmoor exercise was an 'enemy' landing on Porlock beach and an attempted advance into the hills. On one occasion a 'bruising battle' ensued when Minehead Home Guard attacked the Dunkery Hotel at Wootton Courtenay which was defended by platoons from Dunster, Timberscombe, Blue Anchor and Cutcombe. 'Fifth Columnists' were sent in to complicate the manoeuvres including one disguised as a Western National bus inspector on a motor-cycle and another dressed as a woman picking worts on the slopes of Dunkery.

Brompton Regis Home Guard
R. Stevens, E. Davey, R. Thomas, E. Howe, J. Hayes, W. Williams, W. Yerbury, R. Hole H.Davey
H. Toye, H. Norman, E. Lock, H. Hayes, H. Evett, R. Gale, J. Hancock, A. Hole, T. Salter, G.Hayes, G. Snell
J. Hawood, E. Colemand, W, Davey, J. Vaulter, J. Parsons, S. Gibbs, C. Snell, L. Norman, W.Lock

Allerford Museum

Exton and Bridgetown Home Guard

Allerford Museum

From the beginning of the war, North Hill, Dunster Beach and much of higher Exmoor – Brendon Common and Martinhoe Common for example – were taken over as training grounds for the military. The hard winter of 1940-41 was hardly conducive to the success of training exercises and in the Exmoor parish church logbook the Rev. George Wardropper Surtees, a somewhat litigious and controversial priest, usefully describes a major troop exercise on the Moor that went badly wrong. Simonsbath, along with other moorland villages within a radius of ten to fifteen miles, were positions to be taken or defended. The exercise was spread over two weeks, with Simonsbath occupied first by an offensive army, and then relieved. 'Thousands of troops of every description, with convoys of guns, buses and lorries passed through the village in each direction.' All went well until a wrong order was given, and before long the roads leading into Simonsbath from South Molton, Challacombe and Exford were blocked solid with stationary traffic.

The first part of the exercise was held in pouring rain while the second was seriously disrupted by a heavy snowstorm that lasted for 24 hours, and sadly ended in tragedy. Hundreds of men in outposts on the moors, encumbered by vehicles, medium range guns, small arms and other equipment, soon realised the danger they were in. They abandoned their equipment in the snow, by then two to three feet deep, and made their way towards safety. By the time they reached the roads many were exhausted and were revived only by the hospitality of nearby farms and cottages. It is believed that seven men died, at least two suffocated by the fumes of a lorry in which they had taken shelter and for warmth kept the engine running.

Early the following week, relays of troops, mainly from the camp at Torrington, came to Exmoor to find and rescue the equipment abandoned on the moors. 'So ended the only "Battle of Exmoor" known to History,' wrote the parson.

On Dunster Beach the holiday chalets were commandeered – first for evacuees and later by the Army who were involved in building and maintaining sea defences and in training. In 1942 the Americans arrived and encamped on Dunster Beach while practising tank manoeuvres and gunnery on North Hill. The latter became a training ground for tanks from 1942 to 1945 and all the upper part of the hill was, naturally, closed to the public. Tank gunnery ranges were constructed, roads made up, some with concrete surfaces and hundreds of tank crews – British,

Canadian and American – were trained using Churchill and Sherman tanks. Towards the end of the war a battalion of Guards was also trained in mortar firing on North Hill. Many thousands of shells were fired and West Myne farmhouse became one of the casualties of the war – it was within the tanks' firing line and at the end of the war only rubble remained.

In 1946 a military working party searched the training area – about 2550 acres – for live explosives and found and destroyed over 600 live shells, mortar bombs and other 'lethal objects'. These were a hazard in many parts of Exmoor and in 1944 the police visited schools to warn children about the 'objects' that they might find on the commons that had been occupied by troops and the Home Guard.

Some parts of Exmoor were used for training the American forces before the D-Day landings. Clare Court in *A Somerset Village in Wartime* describes how in 1944 the American army arrived quite without warning. 'Sylvia Carpenter, cycling to her job at the food office in Williton one April morning was surprised to meet a convoy of heavy American army vehicles driving up Abbey Road in Washford,' she writes. Val Hole, as a young lad in Roadwater, watched a seemingly endless stream of trucks and jeeps roll through the village making their way to Brendon Hill, just one of the areas where they were billeted. The soldiers were made very welcome at Roadwater, the village hall committee threw the hall open to the visitors and during the next few weeks the village buzzed with action. Dances were held once or twice a week and the Americans played baseball on Roadwater's cricket ground. 'And the outstanding feature throughout their stay was the friendliness between them, our own troops and the civilian population,' reads the village hall annual report. And then, almost as suddenly as they had arrived, they were gone.

Exmoor Ponies

Until the advent of the tractor and motor car the Exmoor pony was a working animal carrying the farmer to oversee his sheep and to market and his children to school; pulling carts, traps and sleds and sometimes being used to draw the plough and haul timber. During the 1940s many were still being used in this way.

But it was also during the 1940s that several horrific incidents led to a catastrophic decline in the number of ponies. Criminal butchers came at night, drove ponies living free on the moor into narrow lanes and stole them away to be slaughtered for meat. Others were killed by American tank and gunnery crews stationed on Exmoor and practising on Brendon Common who used them for target practice. A further problem was that with the coming of the motor car gates onto the moor were constantly left

Brendon Two Gates, 1930s. Gates left open allowed stock to stray

Alfred Vowles

open – there were no cattle grids – ponies strayed and so some farmers decided it was better to keep them in fields near the farms rather than on the open moorland. Another wartime problem was the absence of many of the young men who normally undertook the active management of the herds. The Exmoor Pony Society may not have been functioning either since no records are available for the period though they may have been lost. As Sue Baker points out in *Survival of the Fittest*, 'Generally, and understandably in wartime, the ponies were not uppermost in people's minds and pony breeding declined.'

By the end of the war there were only about fifty purebred free-living Exmoor ponies left. It was only the hard and dedicated work of individuals like Mary Etherington, the daughter of the Rector of Withypool; the scientist, James Speed whom she later married, and members of the Exmoor Pony Society that saved the breed. Miss Etherington persuaded local farmers to put every effort into breeding the ponies and rebuilding the herds and also helped campaign for the introduction of cattle grids to restore the integrity of the commons and allow farmers to restock them with both sheep and ponies.

Tarr Steps Farm, the home of Mr and Mrs Edwin Vowler 1939-45

Farming
Whatever else, the war boosted farming on Exmoor, for the need for homegrown food was paramount. The War Agricultural Committee demanded that areas of rough moorland full of gorse and heather should be ploughed and potatoes planted where no crops had been grown before. Later some of this land was used for root crops, some seeded for grass and some for corn. As part of this scheme more than 2000 acres were ploughed for the first time on the top of the Brendons between Heath Poult Cross and Raleigh's Cross.

Many men had left to join the Forces and Land Girls became an essential part of the workforce. Florence Hall talked to me some ten years ago now and told me how she was parlourmaid to Sir Edward and Lady Malet at Chargot at Luxborough before she joined the Women's Land Army in 1942. On her first day she was taken to moorland on the top of Elworthy Barrows on the Brendons. 'It was pouring with rain, cold and a dense fog. We were given staff hooks and told to cut the heather and gorse bushes off at ground level. It was very tough work. Blisters appeared on our hands and we soon found out where our muscles were. We had to dig the small thorn bushes out but tractors were used to pull out the larger bushes. All the bush stuff had to be burnt on the hills because a special wide plough (which we called a Prairie Buster) was used to plough up this moorland and there was great activity with us cutting and burning, followed by the plough, rollers and cultivators and

Land Army Girls outside their hostel at Williton

Exmoor Photographic Archive

then rollers again. The next year the moor was ready for corn sowing.'

Fine crops of cereals were harvested on the hills for just two years during the war following exceptional summers but then bad weather made harvesting impossible. The demands of the War Ag. caused annoyance and frustration to many of Exmoor's farmers, compelled to plant cereals and potatoes on land they knew to be unsuitable. There was much opposition and shaking of heads but if farmers categorically refused to co-operate they were removed from their farms. Such farms were then run directly by the War Ag.

John Stoate, local spokesman for the National Farmers' Union, spoke out: 'On the hills you have the best views and the poorest harvesting. Hundreds of acres of corn on our hill-country have not been cut and never will be because it is impossible. We are not against ploughing up orders, but we are concerned at being told to grow corn in areas which are not suitable.' It was only after the corn harvest failed that farmers were encouraged instead to improve their land for grass and food for livestock, something which some would continue to do, with Government help, when the war was over.

In 1941 a government subsidy was introduced to encourage hill farmers to keep more sheep with another two years later for beef cattle. Earlier subsidies had encouraged lowland farmers to enlarge their dairy herds and there was also an increase in the number of beef cattle being sent onto Exmoor for summer pasturing. By the time war broke out many farmers, especially in the vales, had invested in tractors but work-horses remained paramount and much loved.

When Vinah Bell came to Exmoor as a Land Girl in June 1948 she found that farming had changed little. She recorded her experiences in the 1996 *Exmoor Review.*

Vinah went to work for Kenneth Baker at South Hill Farm, Withypool where the Bakers worked as a family with no set hours, each with certain responsibilities but all chipping in at busy times to get the jobs done. First up put the kettle on the hot plate! Mrs Baker did most with the poultry, but when needed Vinah helped wash eggs, plucked and drew the birds, and shared the cleaning out of the henhouses with Mr Baker. The cows were hand-milked and the calves fed before breakfast. Milk was put into pans that stood until the cream rose to the top and then were brought nearly to the boil. Next day the clotted cream was skimmed off and sometimes sold.

After breakfast they saw to the sheep, in summertime keeping a daily eye for fly strike and for foot rot all the year round. When the sheep were turned out on the moor, somebody rode out once a day to see them. During lambing they took it in turns alternate nights to go out several times armed with a Tilley lamp. Only in very bad weather did they bring any sheep indoors and then usually after they had lambed. In winter and spring the cows and older bullocks were turned out on the moor by day but they always came home at night. Occasional strays had to be fetched home.

Willie Buckingham bringing in hay at Molland, 1940.
Exmoor Photographic Archive

Relaxing after haymaking at Molland. The Buckingham family of Pulworthy Farm, 1940.
Exmoor Photographic Archive

The man who did the castrating toured the district doing all the calves at the same time. M&B was just becoming available but most treatments were the old ones: for mastitis they rubbed the udder with bacon fat. The doctor came once a week and held surgery in the front room. Cuts and bruises were of no consequence – they just rubbed or bandaged them and got on with the work.

The horses included Toby, the hunter; Peter, a light workhorse and Joey, a wonderful old Exmoor ridden by Mrs Baker. Later came Pixie, an Exmoor bought at Bampton Fair that Vynah broke in and learned to ride.

'We had a couple of hives in the orchard. I used to help by holding the skep to catch the swarms, and with the extraction of the honey in the autumn. We lived well, what with the honey and clotted cream. In the winter a pig was killed and salted, giving us bacon, ham and salted joints. We grew potatoes, also turnips, swedes, and kale for the cattle and sheep, but equally tasty in the house. Eggs, ducks and chicken all found their way on to the table, and sometimes Mr Baker and I shot a rabbit for the pot. Milk, of course was ad lib.

'A strip of woodland belonged to the farm. When the trailer for the tractor began to fall to pieces, we went and felled some trees, sawed them into planks and rebuilt the trailer ourselves; this was still the period when we made do and mended. All bar the plough and the transport box for the Ferguson were converted from horse-drawn equipment. The only grain crop we grew was oats. We scythed round the field first, ready for the crop to be cut by a binder, while there was some green in it. The sheaves were stooked in the field to dry and ripen, and then fed to the bullocks unthreshed. One terribly wet year when it started to sprout in the stook, we hammered six-inch nails round the Dutch barn, hanging the sheaves up to dry. We also used tripods to make hay, stacked them in the barn, leaving the doors open.

'When the snow came, we made sledges to take the hay round and for

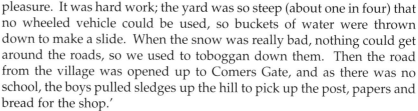

Horses were the main source of power on Exmoor farms throughout the 1940s. Crystal Earl driving the horse rake at East Anstey, 1940.

Exmoor Photographic Archive

pleasure. It was hard work; the yard was so steep (about one in four) that no wheeled vehicle could be used, so buckets of water were thrown down to make a slide. When the snow was really bad, nothing could get around the roads, so we used to toboggan down them. Then the road from the village was opened up to Comers Gate, and as there was no school, the boys pulled sledges up the hill to pick up the post, papers and bread for the shop.'

The 1940s are remembered as the last decade when snow brought life on the moor to a halt nearly every year and 1947 was particularly bad with many people being snowed in for nearly three months. At Withypool the weekly Saturday bus was unable to get through for nine Saturdays in succession. During the snows of January 1945 the head teacher at Withiel Florey noted not only the poor attendance in the face of 'the grip of Arctic weather' but also that bread and butcher's meat was being delivered by army lorries and that the 'dinner van' which kept trying to get through had finally given up having collided with a lorry. Drifts were between six and ten feet deep.

Village Survey 1947

In 1947 a survey was made into the amenities of Somerset villages; a survey which was, I believe, linked with reconstruction after the war. The questionnaires were generally sent to the head teacher of the village school or, if there were no school, to the rector. The survey enquired into the provision of utility services such as water, electricity and sewage. Further questions were asked about shopping and public transport, venues for public meetings, and the incidence of societies, clubs and entertainment.

Lizzie Baker, postwoman, Cutcombe Post 1947. Posties often had a walking round of up to 16 miles.

Kingsley Taylor (Allerford Museum)

The results of the survey are not really surprising. Larger places such as Porlock, Dulverton, Lynton and Lynmouth plus a few villages sited strategically on the B roads usually had a piped water supply and often electricity provided by a local company. Several of these villages had main drains provided by the Rural and Urban District Councils. However in the smaller and more isolated parishes there were few, if any, such services and those that there were tended to depend on local landlords and private enterprise.

Mains electricity only reached the furthest outposts of Exmoor within the last few years. In the 1940s electricity was provided in many places by private companies like the Exe Valley Electricity Company that supplied Brushford and Dulverton and the early hydro-electric scheme that supplied Lynton and Lynmouth. On farms there was often a generator but back in the 1940s most people in the country were cooking on solid fuel ranges while their homes were lit by oil lamps and candles.

Wells were commonplace on Exmoor and many people were served by a piped supply from a local source that often ran dry in summer. Some villages relied on stand pipes or private pumps. Outside the front door of South Hill Farm at Withypool was a well from which water was pumped for cooking and drinking. River water was pumped up from the Barle to a tank above the house for all other uses. Eventually a dowser came to find the head of the spring, and a tank was built where the water came out of the rocks to supply the house. Although there were small reservoirs supplying water locally like those at Nutscale and on North Hill, neither Clatworthy nor Wimbleball Reservoirs existed.

There were proper sewerage systems in Minehead but many places with flush lavatories relied on a cesspit. The norm for cottagers was still the privy or earth closet down the garden; the waste was cleared weekly and often used on the vegetable patch where it helped to produce fine crops of cabbages, carrots and cucumbers. At some of the farms privies had been constructed over water leats in earlier centuries and from these the waste was carried cleanly away on to the fields. Very occasionally the only facility was a plank over a stream or pond with the waste going straight into the watercourse. Apart from these extremes it should be pointed out that most privies were kept spotless and lime-washed at least once a year while cinders, leaf mould or earth, sometimes with added lime, was sprinkled into the privy after use.

There were small general stores and post offices in many villages but people relied for their supplies of bread, groceries, meat and fish on delivery vans. At Clatworthy, for example, in 1947 there were two grocery deliveries, one of meat and two of bread during the week and delivery vans from Dulverton, Bampton, Wiveliscombe and King's Brompton all called weekly at Skilgate. Milk and cream were bought from nearby farms.

The survey's questions seemed irrelevant in many of Exmoor's isolated communities. In his response, the Rev. A. E. Taylor, Rector of Oare and Culbone, explained that the parishes of Oare and Culbone consisted of just a few farms and cottages for land-workers. 'All the people (only a small number) are busy with farm work and taking in paying

Janice Earl clearing snow at East Anstey, 1947.

Exmoor Photographic Archive

When mains electricity came to Exford, SWEB displayed electrical equipment in a marquee on the village green.

Allerford Museum

*Ella Steel delivers milk from Lower
Moor Farm, Minehead.*

Porlock Museum

guests and supplying teas to visitors, so it is difficult to fill in your form
for this district. We have no village, no shop, no post office & no pub.
Brendon some three miles away has PO & shops (one or two) & has a
larger population. Some of our farms are not easily reached unless by
horseback or by a long walk. Much of my time is taken up with visitors
or getting about the farms.'

Three years later in December 1950, when a follow-up questionnaire
was sent, Mr Taylor, somewhat exasperated, enlarged on the situation.
'This is not the ordinary kind of parish. It has no village I'm glad to say,
it's a moorland farm district with scattered farmhouses and cottages and
practically everyone takes in guests. It's a holiday district.

'Lynton and Lynmouth tradesmen call round every week and many
people shop at Porlock and Minehead. There are very few children in the
parish. The charm of Exmoor is its great, wide, open spaces. We have
very large dances & socials & whist parties here; folk come from all over
the Moor. Every farm has many sheep. It's a sheep district. Dr
Nightingale of Lynton is the doctor and a chemist calls every week from

Lynton. Tradesmen from Porlock also call. In summertime there is a good bus service, fewer run in winter but there's a daily service between Minehead and Lynmouth.

'The other parish is Culbone in the Ashley Combe Estate belonging to Lord Knebworth. This parish has a few scattered sheep farms. His lordship has a large nursery of forest trees. He has a fully licensed Residential Centre at Ashley Lodge & another at Culbone Stables which is non-residential for farmers with hundreds of members (fully licensed). Crowds of buses and motor-touring coaches come to the parish every day some six months of the year. I hope this will enable you to see that these parishes are quite out of the ordinary country village parish. Both churches are visited by thousands of persons every year.' Mr Taylor does his best to answer a questionnaire that he clearly considers irrelevant but nonetheless you get the feeling that his message is really to go away and stop asking silly questions.

Over at Simonsbath the head teacher, Miss Barralet, obviously felt much the same but tried to be more positive. 'Many of the homes have no road. Simonsbath is not sufficiently populated to form any societies – there could be a community centre provided that it could be organised so all ages could be catered for. There is decided interest and latent talent in music, drama, and dancing but regular meetings are difficult owing to long journeys, and difficult country and very rough weather. As Head Teacher I should like to stress that after leaving school at the early age of 14, or 15 years, there is no opportunity for any further education or cultural interests. A certain number of inhabitants are concerned with the Exmoor Foxhounds and there is a small group who meets during the winter months for Rifle Shooting practice. A bi-weekly bus service to South Molton would be a great asset, here it is possible to get a further service to Barnstaple.'

In most villages the social high spots were whist drives and dances. During the war these were often laid on by local organisations in aid of the Red Cross or Comforts for Soldiers and in Dunster the WI organised dances, whist drives and films every month. One land girl remembered: 'We had a wireless; used to listen to the Saturday play, putting the set on the windowsill between the bedrooms. We turned out, whatever the weather, for village hops. We had a violinist and a pianist; the post-mistress always sang *Buttons and Bows*, while a notice outside the hall said "no hobnailed boots allowed".'

In 1947 there were cricket and football teams in many villages and, of course, hunting continued throughout the war, for deer and foxes on the moor still needed to be culled.

The Exmoor Accordion Band, 1950 Left to right: Harold Hunt, Stan Curtis, Johnny James and Roger Nicholls.

Stan Curtis

(Above) Miss Abbott, of The Cottage, Dulverton and (right) Master of the Devon and Somerset Staghounds 1940-1951 was, according to Dick Lloyd, a wonderful character, highly intelligent and much loved. During the war she was fully involved with the Observer Corps and used to spend the nights on the top of Exton Hill, plane spotting, after a hard day's hunting.

Allerford Museum

In spite of the war Exmoor was 'full of holidaymakers' in the 1940s. Visitors stayed in local farmhouses and cottages and enjoyed the beauty of the moor and the good food on offer. Some people returned year after year to stay with the same family, often establishing long-lasting friendships. In his seminal work *Exmoor*, S. H. Burton recounted how he fell in love with Exmoor at first sight finding 'a new world, a liberating freedom' in its magnificence and its intimacy. Other visitors, according to his guide and mentor, HB, arrived on Dunkery by charabanc, marched in a noisy crowd to the top, climbed all over the cairn, dropped sweet papers in the heather, carved their initials on the memorial stone and then 'say they have seen Exmoor. They can't be quiet and they haven't learnt to see.'

By the end of the 1940s change on Exmoor must have seemed inevitable. Improved farm technology, common ownership of the motor car, uninhibited tourism, unlimited housing development – all were potential threats to Exmoor's integrity and only a relatively small area of the moor was protected through its ownership by the National Trust. What if Exmoor should become a National Park?

Visitors look forward to tea on Selworthy Green.

Exmoor Photographic Archive

PART TWO

THE ORIGINAL
EXMOOR VILLAGE

A GENERAL ACCOUNT BY
W.J. TURNER

BASED ON FACTUAL INFORMATION FROM
MASS OBSERVATION

WITH PHOTOGRAPHS BY
JOHN HINDE

Introduction to the Original Edition
OUR METHOD

THIS is the first of a series of books whose intention is to present rather more fully, and in a new manner, people and their various ways of life.

Such a presentation cannot be complete and comprehensive, for it would then lack art and become an indigestible mass of facts. Selection of some sort is absolutely essential, and yet an attempt to give a picture that contains the most individual and revealing features must also be made.

To make the volumes as distinct and purposeful as possible the subject of each has been selected as representing a small group, or self-contained community, that is also, however, in its way, typical of similar examples elsewhere, making up the life of larger areas. Naturally no particular small group can in all respects provide a true sample of all the similar collections in the country, yet it was felt that a detailed close-up study of a small group would be of greater value than a more diffused account such as would inevitably result from an attempt to cover an immediately wider field.

Every effort has been made to present authentic and accurate surveys and to express the outlook and feelings of the people described; nevertheless, occasional comment has not been withheld, and there is much that is novel in the manner of presentation of the information obtained.

Just as in recent years sound and colour have been added to the film, widening its scope and enlarging its appeal, so also in modern book production the use of charts and photographs, both in colour and in black and white, has become of ever greater importance. But these books are not primarily 'picture-books', or just a text with illustrations, they are the result of an attempt to coordinate the work of a number of specialists working in harmony and according to plan in the concerted attempt to produce a whole.

For instance, in the present case a detailed report compiled by the independent social research organisation Mass-Observation has formed the basis of the facts about the villagers, their domestic interiors, their activities, and their social relations with one another. Mass-Observation is a scientific, fact-finding body, founded in 1937 to study the habits, behaviour, and opinions of ordinary people. For the purposes of this book their observers lived for some time on the spot, inconspicuously and in varying roles. Their practice is not to resort to formal interviewing, but to gather information in a slow, roundabout way which gives a truer insight.

Mass-Observation has made many surveys of this description, though few have yet been published. Mr Tom Harrisson, its Director, says:

> It has been a real pleasure to work with people who understand both the social facts and the human stuff behind them, who realize that scientific material can be humanly handled without pedantry and with artistry. Numerous social surveys and other such research documents are full of real live facts about real live people, but in print appear flat, lifeless, difficult to assimilate, and suitable only for the specialist. The collaboration of author, skilled observer, photographer, and printer can make a great difference, giving added significance out of all proportion to the extra work and teamwork involved.

The photographer also lived in the village, and the photographs used in the book are selected from a considerably greater number taken at the time. The addition of colour to the black-and-white photographs is not in order to make pretty pictures, or to relieve monotony, but to bring home to the reader in the most vivid manner possible the precise nature and appearance of the people and their surroundings. In addition to conveying what might be described as 'detail atmosphere' the colour illustrations are sometimes used to provide information largely dependent upon colours – as, for instance, the character of the local building materials.

W.J.T.

PLATE I   *Luccombe: Looking North-west to the Bristol Channel.*

PLATE II   *A Village interior.*

PLATE III   *Mr and Mrs Keal at home in Porch Cottage*

PLATE IV   *Mrs Keal.*

Rose Cottage, Stony Street.

Council House, Stony Street.

Miss Sims's House and the Village Shop.

Cloutsham Farm.

The Village School.

Farm Building at Luccombe.

PLATE V

PLATE VI   *Picking Whortleberries on the Moor.*

PLATE VII   *Mrs Gould talking with Mrs Tame on the steps of her house.*

PLATE VIII   *The Village Shop.*

PLATE IX   *Mrs Gould.*

PLATE X   *Work at the Sawmill at Horner.*

PLATE XI   *Mr Moore, the woodman, felling a tree in the Tivington Woods.*

PLATE XII   *Mr Keal in his Allotment with his Grandaughter Winifred.*

PLATE XIII   *Scything in Luccombe Churchyard.*

PLATE XV   Luccombe Mill Farm.

PLATE XIV   Mr and Mrs Strong at Luccombe Farm.

PLATE XVI
*Mr Strong of Luccombe
Mill Farm.*

PLATE XVII *Edward Keal, who works
at West Luccombe Farm.*

PLATE XVIII *Edward Keal pegging
thatch.*

PLATE XIX *Alfred Keal, Foreman ay
Ley Farm.*

PLATE XX *Mr Clarke of West
Luccombe Farm.*

PLATE XXI
*Threshing at West
Luccombe Farm.*

PLATE XXII (left)
*Mr Clarke of West
Luccombe Farm dress-
ing sheep.*

PLATE XXIII (right)
*The local thatcher at
work preparing pegs.*

PLATE XXIV   *'The Square,' showing the Lych Gate and the Keals' Cottage.*

One

THE ENGLISH AGRICULTURAL VILLAGE

FOR more than a thousand years the majority of people in the British Isles have lived by agriculture – cultivation of the land. During that period there have been an enormous number of small yearly material and psychological changes which, added together, have in many ways transformed the life of the people – incidentally welding an aggregate of tiny primitive communities into a modern nation. Yet certain basic activities have not radically changed and the life of an agricultural village in England still resembles – very closely in some respects – what it was in the twelfth century. Life in any English city today would be in every particular unrecognizable to a man of the twelfth, or even the sixteenth, century, but not so life in many an agricultural village. This is particularly true of some parts of the English country. England is not a large country, but it is exceptionally diversified in its physical character, and it contains only a few areas of flat country, mainly in the Midlands, East Anglia, and Lancashire. There is nothing comparable to the vast plains of Northern and Eastern Europe and their enormous agricultural estates. The land is broken up into high moors, deep valleys and abrupt mountainous tracts. Large parts of Wales, Somerset, and Devonshire are steep, hilly country. Then there are the South Downs, the Lake District, the deep Derbyshire valleys, and the moors of Yorkshire. Every few miles in three-quarters of England the country changes in character, sometimes quite radically. This broken, diverse nature of the country has made for diverse ownership and comparatively small estates and small farms. All this has favoured individuality and the development of difference rather than sameness. It also hampers large-scale methods and the quick adoption of novelties and is favourable to conservatism, permanence, and the stubborn adherence to tradition. At a time in the world's history when we are witnessing a quick and steady deterioration in so many directions, we may be inclined to be thankful that Nature has here put a check on the tendency to degradation which exists in mankind along with the desire to improve.

In this Exmoor village we may see country life very much as it was hundreds of years ago. The church is still the centre of the village as it was in the fourteenth century and earlier; whereas in our big cities, and especially in their suburbs, the churches have lost all character and importance (with a few exceptions due to the personality of individuals). In the old English village church we can always find traces of the most important social changes, such as the Reformation, the Civil War, the rise of Nonconformity, and the Evangelical Movement. The West Country cathedrals are veritable local museums and histories of the past – not excluding the country's foreign wars and the development of the Empire and the Dominions overseas. An agricultural village is the only example left of the old community life based on the twin powers of Church and State, but although the village remains, the communal life has dwindled from what it was. It has become at the same time less important and more strictly personal. It has probably changed more in the last fifty years than ever before owing to (*a*) the vast importation of foreign food and (*b*) the development of transport. Wheat from Canada and Australia; butter from Denmark, Australia, and New Zealand, and meat from North and

South America have sapped the strength and independence of the farmers, and motor transport has revolutionized the habits of centuries, dissolving local ties and uprooting families more thoroughly even than wars.

Many of these changes will be for the better ultimately, but the period of transition is often apt to be more disruptive than beneficial; there is here, as everywhere else, the conflict between short- and long-term advantages. Few would deny the immense material benefits, yet the ordinary way of life has suffered and in some respects deteriorated. There is less character and less individuality now in the country village because there are fewer active craftsmen. The village has, in fact, lost its aristocracy and become more of a proletariat, so the distinction between urban and country men is rapidly diminishing. It has been left without direction. Its ancient leaders, the lord of the manor and the rector of the church, have faded or are fading out of the picture, their natural functions gone. But they have left nothing in their place except the ravings or wisdom of the daily newspapers competing for the villagers' pennies. The political campaigns of these rivals mean very little to the villager. They hardly seem to touch on his vital interests. He does not even know where his vital interests lie, for he is likely to find the 'circuses' of the city as seductive in prospect as the townsman has found them devitalizing in effect. Nobody can doubt that the general dissatisfaction with what life has come to be in all its meaninglessness prevailing not only in England but all over Europe today, is a sign of a coming fundamental change. But some of the things which all men desire were once to be enjoyed more in our Exmoor village than they are anywhere in town or country today; and this description of things as they are in our village may throw some light on what is needed for the future.

Two
A First Impression

ON our first evening at Luccombe we drove up to Webber's Post, the name given to the neck of land leading on to Dunkery Beacon. The road follows a narrow ridge overlooking the Horner and Cloutsham valleys, which are magnificently wooded. Looking down on them, we could not see the stream and path at the bottom of the valley because of the closeness of the trees. It was like looking down on to cloud from a mountaintop, only here the rolling clouds were of every variety of green, magnificently lit by the sun. Across the valley the land rises steeply to Porlock Hill and on to Exmoor. Following down this line of hills, we looked over the little town of Porlock to the sea, then across the seaward mouth of the valley to Minehead Hill. Behind us lay Luccombe; straight ahead Dunkery Beacon.

Under the group of pines at Webber's Post the National Trust have already set up a collecting box and a list of prohibitions. So far there is nothing either inviting or informative in their notices. Up at Webber's Post we got the feeling very clearly of Luccombe's immediate hinterland. Miles and miles of moorland, heather and gorse and whortleberries; an occasional remote hill farm but otherwise nothing. Exmoor lies to the south of Luccombe, and it was therefore from this side that we approached the village this evening, coming down off the moor by a track which drops down very steeply through woods. It is a wide stony track overhung with trees – oaks, ashes, and rowans – and beside it is a deep gulley carrying a stream down to the village; ferns and mosses grow over the boulders and up the sloping trunks of the trees.

Luccombe is T-shaped, and we followed the track down into Stony Street, which is the stem of the T. The village runs up to the edge of the wood, and Stony Street itself, which begins with two cottages standing rather isolated from the village, is merely a continuation, widened a little and with a metalled surface, of the track off the moors. The two cottages standing together at the top of the street immediately give the feeling of the village. The moor is behind them; in front of them opens the fertile valley. They are the colour of clotted cream or country butter; the thick thatch and round tall chimneys give an impression of warmth and domesticity. The first house has a porch and a couple of steps up to the open door; the wireless is turned on for the news. Very often the morning papers arrive in Luccombe after the six o'clock news, for there is no delivery, and the papers are brought out by one of the villagers who works in Porlock as a gardener and carries them back with him on his bicycle when he comes home from work. Not every cottage has a wireless and not all of them take a paper. But in the first cottage in Stony Street the wireless is on. Here lives Mr Moore, the woodman of the Holnicote Estate, who has been felling trees in the Tivington woods, towards Minehead. His old father still works most days for the estate as a mason's labourer. In a village like Luccombe, which still draws its livelihood from the land, those who work – and only the very old, the very young, and the infirm do not work – work with their hands. There are, of course, other exceptions, but they are outside the real village community. The parson, for instance, the schoolmistress, and the two old ladies who used to be summer visitors and finally built a house here and settled down; they have never become part of the village for the very reason that their lives are not concerned with it.

Walking down the street, savouring the air and light, one realizes that, however much photographs show, they (like our maps) never show enough, and they cannot convey the coolness and freshness of the air, nor the gentle declivity of the street. The stream which we followed from the hill runs beside the road, and a handrail has been put up to prevent people from slipping down into the deep gulley. After a hundred yards the trees end and the rest of Stony Street opens before you. All the houses are on the left of the street, with the stream on the other side, and this gives an unexpected sense of openness, as though it were an esplanade, and the rail a sea wall where you can lean and talk and watch the evening darken.

In the first house lives Mrs Gande with her three children. She came from Bow, in London, early in the war, and her husband has been in the Army. The children go to the Luccombe school, and the whole family have been accepted remarkably quickly by the village, which, like all small communities, usually takes a very long time to get accustomed to, much more to like, a stranger.

The next two houses are modern council cottages and are set back from the road. This is a good thing because, instead of building in the local style, the council has put up the inevitable semi-detached rough-cast boxes which are without the slightest trace of character or particular local appropriateness. They are not in the least offensive, but they are out of character. All the other houses open straight on to a short flight of steps leading directly into the street. This gives a sense of participation and neighbourliness, so that anyone going up the street is observed and greeted or commented upon. But immediately a house is set back from the road, with a high bank cutting it off from those in the street, the sense of friendly intercourse is broken.

Beyond the two council houses is one standing on its own where Mr Shopland lives with his son, Jimmy. His house is typical of the village, and the photographs attempt to give a complete picture of it. But what they cannot give is the quality of light, the sudden glance out of the window on to fields and trees, the view to the moor. The camera looks at things with a fixed stare, and can give all the documentary evidence – the pattern of the wallpaper, the ornaments on the mantelpiece, the position of the furniture – but it cannot give the background conversation, the broken fragmentary impressions gathered by a roving human eye looking sometimes deliberately and curiously and sometimes idly and unthinkingly over objects and colours and faces. Yet, looked at imaginatively, they can give a good deal of evidence to the stranger who wants to see what is familiar to his own way of life and what is alien to it. They do give, as no amount of information can give, an accurate account of real everyday objects and surroundings.

Both Mr Shopland and Jimmy work with horses, one on Mr Partridge's farm and one at Huntscote. Horses still predominate over machines in this part of the world, and certainly up at a hill farm, like Ley Farm, horses are a good deal more manoeuvrable than machines. The road up to Ley Farm from the Porlock road, for example, would be impossible for a combined harvester: the pitch is terrifically steep and the surface both rough and loose. There is not a single fully-trained mechanic in the village – apart perhaps from the haulier – but there are three carters, and every man and boy in Luccombe must be able to handle horses. Mr Tame is another carter; he works at Blackford Farm and lives with his wife in Porch Cottage, next to the Shoplands. Their nearest neighbours down the street live in a group of three cottages. These three cottages are the very hub of Stony Street. Steps lead down from the front doors, and bushy, flowering hydrangeas grow up against them. A good deal of conversation goes on from these steps, and all the village gossip is exchanged here.

Where Stony Street joins the Porlock–Wootton Courtney road it widens out into what is called the 'Square': it is the official centre of the village. The Keals' cottage faces on to it, and their door stands open and leads straight into the living-room. There is a deep porch and bright flowers in pots grow there, and a large brass tap very brightly polished catches the light at one side. Inside Mrs Keal's cottage it is cool and dark, although the fire is burning and it is a hot sunny day outside. There is an old dark pewseat against the wall and a china dresser covered with mixed china which is gay and shining even in the rather dim light. The mantelpiece is thick with horse brasses and brass ornaments of every description, and each one is as brightly polished as it possibly can be. A low beam runs the length of the house, hung for half its length with jugs of every size and shape and colour. It is Mrs Keal's ambition to have enough jugs to hang all along it.

Opposite the Keals' cottage, on the other side of Stony Street, is the village shop run by Mrs Baker. Against the side wall of the shop there is a little sunken patch of stones where water from the stream evidently drains down, and growing there, is a patch of mullein, or yellow musk, brilliantly yellow and smelling of spice and honey; Mrs Keal had never noticed it before and didn't know what it was. The Keals' house backs on to the churchyard, and the lych-gate is at right angles to their doorway. There is also a way in from Stony Street at the south corner of the church-yard, and along the wall which runs down to the end of the street grows an old row of cypress trees which look strange and Italianate in this English village.

To walk down Stony Street as we did on that first evening, knowing beforehand how all the people lived, made us realize how much the land itself still matters. Every man who lives in Stony Street works out of doors every day of his life, and mostly when he comes home in the evening he works on in his garden or on his allotment till darkness comes. Most of the boys growing up want to work on the farms like their fathers. Most of the girls will marry men of this village or some neighbouring parish. The women are inevitably more indoors, but a single step from the front door and they are looking at country a townsman travels hundreds of miles to see. And country people do not grow indifferent or blasé. They notice and enjoy the changing lights and seasons. Luccombe lies on the edge of the fertile Porlock valley, and at its back stretch all the miles of wild moorland; so that often in the evening you can walk up through the plantation of pine and larch trees to the edge of the heather and surprise a group of deer from the covert where they have been lying up all day. High fences have to be put round the fields to keep them from the crops. Stag-hunting on Exmoor is one of the great events, and there is hardly a cottage in Luccombe which has not got some trophy from a past hunt.

Running at right angles to Stony Street, and at its juncture forming the 'Square', is the main road from Wootton Courtney, which breaks up at the 'Square' into the two main roads travelling north-westward to Porlock and north-eastward to Minehead. Luccombe lies in an enclosed sheltered valley, and the only approach from the west is through the gap in the hills at Wootton Courtney, which is a fairly sophisticated village, a centre of the Exmoor Hunt and apparently rather laid out for visitors with a new hotel which has a magnificent site but is a hideous building. There are several shops, a church, and quite a number of residential houses. It is actually the nearest village to Luccombe, but Luccombe men prefer to go down to one of the inns at Porlock rather than to Courtney.

Halfway up the hill that leads out of Luccombe towards Wootton Courtney a track branches off to the left and leads on to Knowle Top. At the top is a hollow dip where old iron workings used to be, now filled with water and overgrown with brambles. From this steep little hill one of the panorama views was taken. It gives a magnificent idea of the spacious fertile valley running down to the sea and of the surrounding and sheltering hills. Even from here Luccombe has almost disappeared. That is one of the most remarkable things about Luccombe: you have only to go about a quarter of a mile or less from it in any direction and it disappears completely. But from Knowle Top you look down on the church with its fine tower and dark cypress trees and up the length of Stony Street, and both seem far away and far below you.

Back on the Wootton Courtney road we descend as steeply as we climbed and come down to the bottom of the hill and to the last house in Luccombe, Luccombe Mill Farm, owned, when we first went to Luccombe, by Mr Strong. The Strongs' farm is off the road to the left – a plain, low, rectangular house facing south, with a long narrow garden stretching between it and the road. Behind the house are the cow-sheds, barns, stables, and outbuildings. Along the side of the garden and the house runs a little stream, and at night you hear the water running all the while. The water in the house comes from a spring and runs perpetually from the tap. A stream running through a house. A brood of small yellow ducklings swim and splash up and down this stream all day long and have to be collected every night. It was here that we stayed, and there were three other visitors besides us – Miss Pierce, who was a great walker and knew all the surrounding country, and Mrs B. and her daughter, Barbara, who was thirteen and at the age when she liked, more than anything, riding the farm horses and milking the cows and carrying the kittens up into the barn, with a novel to read, and generally keeping every one lively and amused.

Beyond the turning to the Strongs' farm we leave Luccombe; the main road climbs steeply again and runs on narrow and winding for one-and-a-half miles to the village of Wootton Courtney.

Three
LUCCOMBE VILLAGE AND THE COMMUNITY

LUCCOMBE is a small compact agricultural community lying at the foot of Dunkery Beacon in the rich vale of Porlock. It is one-and-a-quarter miles off the main Minehead–Porlock road, and therefore has little through traffic beyond an occasional vehicle from Wootton Courtney to Porlock. But this road is narrow, winding and rough in places, so that through traffic from Wootton usually goes through Tivington to the main road.

The houses and buildings of Luccombe are built along two roads which are at right angles to one another, and whose junction is commonly called the 'Square'. Stony Street, so named because for many years it was rough and stony, extends up as far as Mr Moore's cottage, Hill Gate. Here the road down which we first came into Luccombe enters the belt of trees and climbs steeply up to the almost treeless waste known as Webber's Post.

The road is metalled as far as Hill Gate. From there up to Webber's Post it is a wide woodland track with an almost vertical drop on one side down to the small stream which passes through Luccombe village, and it is from springs in these woods that Luccombe draws its water-supply. We walked up along this track in the direction of Webber's Post one evening and came upon the spring which feeds the village. It flows along a wooden channel into a little brick reservoir, and when this is full the wooden trap-gate is raised and the stream flows on its course down the hill and through the village.

Roads from Porlock, Minehead, and Wootton Courtney join at Luccombe. The Wootton–Porlock road passes over the stream and bears round sharply to the left, following the high stone wall which encloses the rectory grounds. Over the bridge and to the right is a rough unmetalled road to Allerford and Holnicote House, which passes Mr Partridge's farm and buildings. Walking from the Square in the direction of this farm, one passes first the school, then the 'hut' (parish room), and finally what remains of the village green. This consists of a wide patch of grass and brambles along the roadside, and is now only used by Tony Hales, who grazes his goat there. Leading off from the village green, and still on the right-hand side, is a cart-track which leads up to the ruins of the old village pound, now full of miscellaneous tins and other rubbish.

Just behind the school playground and still visible from the road are the few remaining ruins of a cottage which stood there many years ago. Several of the older inhabitants remember a row of cottages once standing over the stream opposite the school, and two cottages have photographs of the main street of Luccombe taken a good half-century ago, showing the row of whitewashed, thatched cottages which stood where the Staddons' and the schoolhouse now are; and showing Mrs Arscott's cottage when it was two thatched cottages. In fact, Luccombe has shrunk slightly during the past fifty to seventy years.

The guidebook facts are these. Luccombe is in the Bridgwater division of the county, the hundred of Carhampton, Petty Sessional division of Dunster, Archdeaconry of Taunton, Diocese of Bath and Wells, and Williton Rural District Council.

Mrs Keal reduces this to everyday human terms: "If you do anything wrong whilst you're here you'll have time to clear out afore we get the policeman from Porlock." The policeman visits Luccombe once a week.

There is a War Reserve policeman living at Horner who is sometimes to be seen, but, as he says, he's "not really a policeman". Luccombe is administered by a parish council, of which Mr Partridge, the farmer, is chairman. It meets irregularly in the village hall when there is anything special to discuss. A representative of Luccombe parish, Mr Broomham, from Doverhay, Porlock, sits on the Williton Rural District Council. The parish of Luccombe has an area of 6945 acres. The population in 1931 was 222. Between March 1932 and April 1944 the parish register shows that there have been forty burials, thirty-nine births, and twenty-three marriages.

These particulars bear out the suggestion already made that Luccombe seems to have shrunk in size, and it is obviously still shrinking. In this it has shared the fate of so many agricultural villages throughout the country and represents that sacrifice of agriculture to industry which has taken place during the last century. Considering that agriculture has been for so long a depressed and restricted way of life, it is even surprising in England that villages like Luccombe are not more backward and uneventful than they are.

Statistically there are thirty-one acres of Luccombe to each man, woman, and child in the community. But ninety-four people (excluding the evacuees at Knap Stables) live in the thirty-one cottages and houses of the village itself. Seven people left during the war for the services, so that about half the population of the parish live within a stone's throw of one another in the village of Luccombe. There are smaller communities in Horner and West Luccombe, and the proportion living in real isolation is very small.

To anyone coming from a big city this compact, tiny community spells peace and quiet. But standards differ, and for one who has lived in the middle of a field, village life may be disconcertingly noisy. The neighbour problem exists in Luccombe just as it does in the flats and semi-detached houses of a city. We had a conversation with Mrs Gould one afternoon, and she said:

> Of course, I didn't always live in the village. I used to live in a little house just outside, and Luccombe was the nearest village. It was right in the middle of a field. Ever so nice, but we had to move. You see, we were only tenants, and they wanted it.
> Prefer it here? No. I preferred it there. It was lovely. When I first got here I couldn't think what it was – neighbours banging away next door. I wasn't used to it, you see. Not after living in the middle of a field.

Mrs Wylde, whose husband is a road-man, lives next door and has three children. One of her problems is that the third bedroom is over the sitting-room of the next-door cottage, and she doesn't feel she should use it for fear of disturbing the neighbours in their sitting-room below. The bedroom is light and pleasant, with windows each end, but the three children sleep in two beds in the second room, while the third is bare of furniture. This neighbourly consideration is typical of most small rural communities. In a town, friends who live a couple of miles apart consider themselves neighbours: in Luccombe, distance is differently measured. Mrs Prescott, thinking of moving thirty yards down the road, complained to us: "The trouble is, I'll miss my friends."

Another example of this parochialism is that of the twenty-three marriages that have been celebrated in the parish within the past twelve years, eleven have been between Luccombe residents; ten have been between Luccombe women and men from outside; one has been between a Luccombe man and a woman from outside; and one was between a doctor from London and a widow who took up residence in Porlock for the purpose of the wedding. Of the ten marriages between Luccombe women and men from outside, six were with men from neighbouring parishes, and the one man who brought a wife to Luccombe from outside brought her only a few miles. In general, marriages within the parish community are common; most Luccombe blood is Somerset blood, and much of it comes from the surrounding parishes.

Of those families who have moved into Luccombe village within the past twelve years, the Strongs came from Bagborough, the Arscotts from Tivington, the Wyldes from Venniford, the Hales from Minehead, the Ambers from Minehead, and the Greigs from near Exford. Other people in the parish, but not in the village, have come from Hawkridge, Cutcombe, and Timberscombe. Of twelve who have left Luccombe, four went to Minehead, one to Yeovil, one to Cutcombe, one to Porlock, one to Washford, one Tiverton way, one to Gloucester, and one to London. Most Luccombe people come from, and go to, places within the neighbourhood.

General view of Luccombe looking west.

Four

HOUSES

THERE are thirty-one houses in and neighbouring the village of Luccombe. Of these, sixteen are detached, twelve are semi-detached and three in a row. To anyone visiting the village for the first time, a striking feature is the thatched roofs. It is easy to come away from Luccombe with the impression that most of the cottages are thatched, and this impression is strengthened by the fact that many of the farm buildings in and around the village have thatched roofs. Actually, of the inhabited houses twenty-one have tiled roofs, seven thatched roofs, and three slate roofs. The majority – twenty of the thirty-one – have walls of pale yellow or cream; seven of red stone, two of grey stone, and two of roughcast.

For interior decoration Luccombe people prefer pastel shades of distemper, and twice as many rooms are distempered as are decorated with wallpaper. An analysis of the interior decoration of the cottages showed:

	Distemper			*Wallpaper*	
Cream	44	rooms	Floral	17	rooms
Green	16	rooms	Modern pattern	9	rooms
Buff	10	rooms	Buff	10	rooms
Yellow	6	rooms	Plain	4	rooms
Whitewash	3	rooms			
Blue	1	room			
Pink	1	room			
TOTAL	81		TOTAL	40	

Cream is far and away the most popular colour for distemper, followed by green, which is used in rather less than half as many rooms. Of the wallpapers, floral patterns are the favourites.

All but seven of the houses can be classified as cottages, and there are twenty-four houses and cottages of the village community proper; these include the houses of the farmers Strong and Partridge, who are an integral part of the village life, and exclude the Rectory, Knap House, Orchard Cottage, and Wychanger, which at present play a relatively small part in the everyday life of the village.

An analysis of living accommodation in the twenty-four village houses shows that:

> 2 cottages have two bedrooms and one living-room
> 1 cottage has three bedrooms and one living-room
> 4 cottages have two bedrooms and two living-rooms
> 11 cottages have three bedrooms and two living-rooms
> 2 cottages have four bedrooms and two living-rooms
> 2 cottages have five bedrooms and two living-rooms
> 2 cottages have four bedrooms and three living-rooms

In these 121 rooms live 74 people, 51 adults and youths and 23 school-children. There are 74 bedrooms, or exactly a bedroom a head, on an average, for each man, woman, and child. Actually, of course, it does not work out like that. Mr and Mrs Prescott live alone in one of the four-bed-roomed cottages, and old Miss Coles and Mrs Baker have two bedrooms apiece and only use one between them. Fred Partridge's seven-roomed farmhouse is included, and he lived alone during the war; and Miss Sims, the schoolmistress, has a five-roomed cottage to herself.

Still, there is no overcrowding in Luccombe. All the cottages are large enough to give the children of each sex a separate room and leave one for the parents. The two three-roomed cottages are occupied respectively by old Mr Gould, and by Mr and Mrs Gould and their children of twelve and nine, and as the children of this family are both girls, there is no over-crowding problem here.

The standard of furnishing, decoration, repairs, and cleanliness in the village is generally very high, especially in those cottages which let rooms to visitors. But there are some individual problems. Mrs Amber's cottage, for instance, has been condemned. During the war her husband was a lorry driver in the Eighth Army. She has two small children and so far she has been unable to find another cottage. She thought her cottage was condemned because it was too near the water, but actually it is perched on the edge of a very steep watercourse and the authorities are afraid of a landslide.

There is sometimes a considerable contrast between the cottages of families which let rooms, and those which do not have people outside the family to stay, for letting brings in extra money for new furniture and small luxuries. One of the cottages we saw, a cottage said to be the oldest in the village and one in which there is no room available for letting, is badly in need of repair. The walls are cracked and need replastering; the furniture is the bare minimum, old and of much poorer quality than is generally found in the village; the two occupied bedrooms contain mere necessities – bed, dressing-table, chest of drawers, and two tin trunks for storing clothes. The wall of one unoccupied room is weak and crumbly, and so is the ceiling – an additional reason for not using it. In the main living-room, along the wall dividing the two downstairs rooms, there is a piece of very old panelling, well-blackened with dust and age, which is said to have been removed at some time from the church. On the walls are a wide variety of pictures and ornaments: a photograph of the Royal Family; the baptismal certificates of the three children, and three certifi-cates which they have won at school – no one knows exactly what for; a large picture in colour of the Devon and Somerset Staghounds crossing the Barle at Tarr Steps, with master, huntsmen, and hounds well to the fore; a large picture of a stag, two small ones of horses, and a number of etchings of different parts of London; two watercolours of old-fashioned water-mills; several framed enlargements of snaps of the children, including one of husband and wife and their eldest son on the day of his christening; a full-plate size photo of the family who lived next door, pre-sented to them on the death of the old lady. The living-room contains the glass-fronted cupboard, full of china and glasses, which is common to most of the cottages here. Water-tap, drain, and earth-closet are all outside.

That is a rough sketch of an interior; less elaborate than some, but nev-ertheless well filled with miscellaneous objects.

The 'front room' is the Luccombe housewife's pride. She fills it with plenty of everything – a large assortment of knick-knacks, several table-cloths, one over the other on the table, innumerable pictures. The floor is full, the wall is full, the cupboards, the mantelpiece, the shelves are full. A typical Luccombe interior reflects various Luccombe interests – hunting, the search for antlers in the woods, the love of flowers, the sea, and the local countryside. Many of the cottages have brass-bound bellows hanging on the wall, and shining brass-work is found in many rooms. A display of brass ornaments is a feature of most Luccombe cottages, and the women take great pride in keeping it well polished; horse brasses are especially popular, but there are many other brass ornaments. One of the best collections is that of old Mrs Keal.

A few years ago Mrs Keal had a leg amputated. Now she sits all day in her chair, crutches leaning against the wall, directing the household like a matriarch. Before she lost her leg she used to go into Minehead regularly to have her hair done and to work daily in the laundry at Allerford. Now she is tied to the village. She looks after 'Granfer' Keal, and their two granddaughters, Nancy Sully, aged sixteen, and Winifred, aged eight. Or rather, in theory, Nancy looks after Grandma. She has a plump, pleasant face, and short iron-grey hair. As we came into the cottage she was knitting a brown sock; new bread was on the table, just baked. She believes she is the only person in the village now who bakes her own bread; she doesn't sell it, but only bakes it for her own household. Her chief worry nowadays is what to give her husband to take away with him in the mornings to eat and she has to get up early in the morning and prepare the food for him to take to Tivington, where he works as a farm labourer. She keeps pigs, however, which helps her out with the meat problem.

Over the fireplace is a collection of brassware, glinting in the sun, and a Prussian helmet has pride of place in the centre. Her husband sent it from France in the First World War; he put it in a box, in bits, and didn't expect it to get home as the men had been told not to send any more. Most of the collection, however, has been found lying around Luccombe at one time and another and carefully polished up.

General view of Porlock looking north from Ley Hill.

Five

THE VILLAGERS

IN the twenty-four cottages which constitute the village community there live twenty-four men and boys, twenty-seven women and girls, and twenty-three schoolchildren. Apart from those still at school, there are about thirty-four people over, and seventeen people under, forty, but this predominance of older people was wholly a war-time feature. There are two households of six, two of five, six of four, three of three, eight of two, and three of one.

Formerly Miss Sims, the schoolmistress, and old Mr Gould were the only two who lived alone, but Mr Partridge had a house to himself after his son joined up. He lost his wife some twenty years ago. Luccombe is very much a village of children, and eleven of the cottages now contain schoolchildren. The two largest families are the Arscotts and the Howards.

The men of Luccombe all work with their hands – with horses, trees, stones, and paint – and in the village there are:

2 carters	1 carpenter
4 farmers	1 labourer at the saw-mills
4 farm labourers	1 mason
2 council roadmen	2 mason's labourers
2 gardeners	1 painter
1 haulier	2 retired men
1 timber cutter	

Life is therefore very much stripped of all superfluities, and most of the questions that are hotly debated in cities and big industrial centres have no interest whatever for Luccombe people as they have more serious business of their own to attend to. There are strictly speaking, therefore, no political opinions or discussions.

Agricultural wages were low before the war, but the standard of living in Luccombe has always been remarkably high. Many factors help: in many ways the village is practically self-supporting, every cottage having its garden, which is kept well stocked by men to whom gardening is second nature; many keep chickens and many keep a pig; rents of 2s.6d. to 3s.6d. a week are common (the two council houses, built fourteen years ago, cost 5s.10d. per week); the temptation to casual spending is strictly limited; there is no pub nearer than Wootton, so that drinking involves a planned expedition; there is no cinema nearer than Minehead. Even then money would have been tight on a pre-war wage for an agricultural labourer with a family. It was, and is, augmented by the women's earnings.

A visitor from London who had not the imagination to realize the vivid agricultural life which goes on behind the mask of quietism might get a dreary impression of the village if undue emphasis were laid on the fact that, of the twenty-four women, two are cripples, one a permanent invalid, and another partially crippled. In addition there is Mrs Keal, who is unable to do anything beyond part of her housework and washing since her leg was amputated, and two of the younger women,

Joan Hales and Nancy Sully, are fully occupied looking after their invalid mother and grandmother respectively. Six of the women are thus either incapacitated or look after invalids. Old Mrs Prescott, who used to let rooms before the war, feels too old for it now; Mrs Rowlands does no other work apart from taking in visitors. Of the remaining women: 8 do some sort of domestic work for other people; 1 helps to wash up and serve school dinners and cleans the school; 2 run the village shop; 1 does dress-making and alterations; 1 is an insurance agent; 1 is schoolmistress at the village school; 1 is a paid assistant at the school is housekeeper to an all-male family, the Moores; 1 is a state-registered midwife, undertaking private cases; 1, though she does no remunerative work, lets rooms and has her function in a doctorless village as a trained first-aider with a St John's certificate. With the exception of the Keal, Hales, and Staddon households, and old Mrs Prescott, every woman in Luccombe is earning some money either by letting rooms, or by doing some occasional work, or both. The occasional work does not bring in a great deal. The commonest occupation is domestic work, and the girls of the village often look forward to going into domestic service when they leave school. Only one of the women, however, has a semi-full-time domestic job. Three are employed by the rectory, one on general housework, one on rough cleaning, and one on cleaning the church. Two work at Knap House, mother and daughter splitting three days between them. Mrs Tame has the only nearly full-time job, five days a week with Mrs Lawrence. The other two are Mrs Bessie Tame, who 'does' for Mr Partridge in the mornings, and Mrs Gould, who does housework in West Luccombe on Wednesdays and Fridays.

One of the pleasantest ways in which the women of Luccombe make extra money is by collecting whortleberries. Exmoor is renowned for its abundant crop of whortleberries, and the inhabitants of Luccombe take full advantage of this free fruit crop. The whortleberry bushes are found in the woods at the top of Stony Street and cover the hill from Webber's Post to Dunkery Beacon. The plant has a small green leaf, and the pink flower, not unlike a miniature Canterbury Bell, appears in early May. The fruit ripens in July and can sometimes still be picked late in September, so it is a long season. The whortleberry, or 'errt', as it is commonly called in Somerset, is a small, dark purple fruit somewhat similar in looks to a fine blackcurrant, but to the urban palate distinctly less tasty. During the season, Luccombe women and children make frequent excursions to the moors. This is a permanent pleasure in their lives year after year and is always equally enjoyed by visitors. Picking 'errts' is a social occasion, and large picnic parties are frequently organized for it. Certain parts of the moor are known by the local people to produce better fruit than others, and naturally they make for these spots. Apart from their household use of it the fruit has a ready sale in other districts, and for many generations the Exmoor people have looked upon the 'errts' as one of their annual harvests. Nowadays lorries come each day to the picking grounds and buy up the fruit at about 2s.6d. per quart, but prices vary slightly with the season, and some dealers buy by weight. During wartime the fruit is valuable as a dye as well as for food. In the old days when agricultural wages were very low the Exmoor cottagers used to rely on the money they received from their whortleberry harvest to provide the whole family with clothing for the coming year.

Most of those who can conveniently do so let rooms to visitors in the spring and summer months. A typical charge is £2.10s.0d. a week, including board, or 7s.6d. a day for short stays. Low enough in comparison with hotel and boarding-house rates, this charge represents a reasonable profit in a village where much of the food is produced at home and where overheads, such as heating, baths, and service, are very small. It is not uncommon for some of the cottages to be booked well ahead in May. There is no advertising to be done – Luccombe housewives depend on personal recommendations and the return, year after year, of old guests – so that another overhead is eliminated. There are often more applications for rooms than rooms available, and the villagers help each other out by letting bedrooms to guests of other cottages.

Luccombe housewives very sensibly do not budget their expenditure, and it is difficult to arrive at an accurate estimate of where the money goes. But, with a wage-earning man in the house, it is not difficult to make ends meet and indulge in small luxuries like an occasional car-ride to Minehead.

A typical country woman of these parts is Mrs Howard, whose husband is a gardener at Porlock. She has a large family to look after and in addition takes in lodgers and washing. Her visitors' book shows an average of nine lots of visitors in a year. In a typical week she washed all day Tuesday; washed and ironed all day Wednesday, and was still ironing at 11pm. She washed a little on Thursday, was ironing nearly all day Friday, and was ironing curtains at 11pm. She had to finish it off on Friday, because she goes out to work on Saturdays. Every day she gets up at 7am, cooks breakfast for the four children and her husband and prepares lunch for Mr Howard to take away. She has a cold meal at 1pm, tea at 4.30, and a hot supper at 7pm. On Saturdays there is a hot dinner at midday, and high tea at 5pm. The Howard family goes to bed later than most of the villagers – about 11.30pm. Mrs Howard's evening's work is interrupted by a putting-to-bed roster – Joan at 9pm, Tony at 10pm, and Basil a bit later. Her house is scrupulously clean. She looks perpetually tired, but never grumbles and is constantly surprised by the energy and excitableness of her children; she is probably the hardest-working woman in the village. Basil goes to Minehead County School, and so fees have to be found as well as other household expenses. Only two other Luccombe children go to fee-paying schools.

The Luccombe women treat their visitors as friends; they enjoy having them as a contact with the outside world, and it is not uncommon for the visitor to invite her hostess to stay in return. What some guests think of Luccombe is found in the comments in prose and verse which they often write in the visitors' book before they leave. At Porch Cottage, Mrs Tame, whose husband is a carter at Blackford farm and who 'does' for old Mrs Lawrence up at Wychanger five days a week from 10.30am to 3.30pm, also manages to take visitors and to give them an excellent reception. The poem in her visitors' book of which she is particularly proud is this one:

> *I lay upon my comfy bed,*
> *The sun shone through the pane,*
> *A knock came on the door, I said*
> *"Is that you, Mrs Tame?"*
> *She brought me in my cup of tea,*
> *It tasted really good*
> *And this was no-wise odd,*
> *because Somehow I thought it would.*
> *Then I arose and wandered far,*
> *And sometimes got home late,*
> *For she's a jolly good fellow –*
> *And you needn't be back 'sharp at eight'.*

From 1931 dates the following piece of verse:

> *If you stay with Mrs Tame*
> *You are sure to come again*

For she lives just down the lane
  Does Mrs Tame
Never were the rooms so clean
While her cooking is a dream
And she lives just by the stream
  Does Mrs Tame
When you come back tired and hot
Tea is ready like a shot
For she's always on the spot
  Is Mrs Tame
Should you crave for worms or string
Books, pills, any mortal thing!
You have only got to ring
  For Mrs Tame.
There's no trouble she won't take
A nice holiday to make
Have you tried the currant cake
  Of Mrs Tame ?
So you'd better book your room
And you'd better do it soon
For she lives in Lucky Combe
  Does Mrs Tame.

and more briefly:

Far from the maddening crowd
Two miles from the nearest pub
But with Mrs Tame it's 'hame from hame'
And she gives you wonderful grub.

Mrs Tame has had many parsons to stay with her, and once an arch-bishop spent his honeymoon at her cottage. One of her clergyman visitors wrote the following poem of which this is merely an extract:

... Mrs Caiger cried "Ahoy!
It's time we moved again, my boy!"
Last year it rained and poured and dribbled
I simply sat at home and scribbled.
Lets hope this time wont come as wet
For we're off to Somerset,
To comfy rooms and lovely scenery
Rolling moors and woodland greenery
Mrs Tame just knows the way
To make a perfect holiday
Get the car and grease it well
Tune it up to go like —
And here's a ton of sweets, we'll suck 'em
As we go rolling back to Luccombe.

          July '32

These verses are some of the less impressive results of compulsory education for all. There is a very different entry by a visitor from Brixton, London, dated October 16, 1940, in the midst of the London blitz:

In these troubled times it has been possible to find peace, perfect peace for a few days at Porch Cottage, thanks to the excellent attention of Mr and Mrs Tame. God willing, I shall return to this haven of rest to take full advantage of all the good things to be found here.

About the prices they charge, the villagers are not communicative, and they do not discuss it among themselves. Letting rooms is not all pleasure, and though the villagers enjoy having visitors on the whole, it sometimes leads to domestic difficulties, and some husbands complain that there is nowhere to sit down when the visitors are about. But the wives say that it is interesting and helps to keep contact with the outside world.

The approach to Luccombe.

Afternoon in Stony Street.

Six

COMMUNICATIONS AND DELIVERIES

THE nearest railway station for passengers is Minehead, and for goods, Dunster. Buses, run by two different companies on alternate weeks, pass Brackley Steps, one-and-a-quarter miles outside the village, on the journey between Minehead and Porlock, ten times a day in each direction, with an afternoon service on Sundays. Some time ago a service operated between the village itself and Minehead, but there were not enough passengers to make it pay. Luccombe is indeed an isolated village to those too old or infirm to walk to Brackley Steps, but most of the women manage to get there fairly regularly.

There are five private telephones in Luccombe, and a call-box was recently installed in the village near the schoolhouse. A pillar-box, set in the wall of Mr Webber's house, is all that remains of what used to be a sub-Post Office before the war. Old Mr Gould still refers to this letter-box as the Post Office. So far as the villagers are concerned the postal arrangements are adequate – one delivery a day and two collections. The postman sells stamps and takes letters for registration; also often collects ordinary letters at the door. From his point of view the arrangements are not so satisfactory. Collections are made by van, the morning delivery taking place on the same trip, and one of the drivers, a Minehead man, complains bitterly of the rush; he starts sorting at 5am and at 8am begins delivery round the villages; he has to be back at 1pm so that the sorters can have the outgoing mail ready for the two o'clock train to London, and executing small commissions for the villagers doesn't leave him much time. However, this was a wartime arrangement. Previously there were three postmen in Allerford who covered all the villages this side of Porlock on foot; Luccombe still comes under Allerford Post Office for the drawing of old-age pensions, etc., but the postal address has been changed to Minehead. All this is the postman's worry, not the villagers. They get their letters and post them with less trouble, if anything, than before.

A rough average for the incoming post to the village of Luccombe is sixty letters a day, outside the visiting season. This includes Wychanger and the rectory – and the rectory gets a big post-bag sometimes – but the postman's impression is that he calls at almost every house each day. The outgoing mail is said to be rather smaller.

Regular deliveries of bread, meat, groceries, fish, and coal are made in the village; three wireless tradesmen call weekly, and two laundries once a fortnight, and in peacetime a representative of a big Minehead shoe retailer calls weekly with a van containing a choice of shoes. So Luccombe is very well served with all the necessities, and it was perfectly possible, even in wartime, for the housewife to keep her larder filled without any outside shopping. For incidentals, there is the village shop, a very small grocery and general store with a cigarette and tobacco licence which depends for its custom entirely on the village. The shop door is divided in two like a stable's, and the bottom half is kept closed. When a customer comes in the cow-bell attached to the door tinkles.

The store is owned by Mrs Baker, aged seventy-eight, who has kept it for over twenty years, and for the past twelve years with her assistant and companion, Miss Coles, who originally came to do the clerical work of the shop. But wartime arrangements have been too much for her; she says she can't manage "the new banking system"; and so once a fortnight someone from the village comes in and "sees to they forms". Money is kept in a little box in a drawer under the counter, for there is no till. Stock is bought, and has been for years, from one man in Taunton; Miss Coles is very severe with him and says she "won't stand any nonsense". Miss Coles, who is over seventy, came from London in response to an advertisement for a companionhelp put into the *Church Times* by Miss Sims, on Mrs Baker's behalf.

The village shop is a centre of gossip, and Miss Coles, wearing a man's checked cloth cap, with the peak cut off, will talk for half an hour with a customer. There are no regular opening and closing hours, but the shop is usually open till dusk.

Back door, Rose Cottage, Stony Street.

Seven

FUEL

THERE is no gas or electricity in the village. Gas ends at Minehead; electricity is supplied at Allerford, and comes as far as Huntscote on the Wootton Courtney road. The nearest electrically lit house to Luccombe is near Huntscote Farm and belongs to an old lady, Miss Stretton, who lives alone in a beautiful cottage which she has had completely modernized and fitted with all the latest electrical devices. In Allerford the village blacksmith has an electrically heated forge, a comparatively rare feature even in districts where equipment is in general more up-to-date. Shoeing is usually done at Allerford as it is more convenient for Luccombe people than Porlock or Wootton. The same blacksmith serves both Wootton and Porlock, spending alternate days at each forge.

Coal is delivered fortnightly to Luccombe by two coal merchants. It is supplemented by logs, which, before the war, were obtainable ready-cut from Holnicote saw-mills and delivered by Mr Prescott, the haulier. Now there are few logs available, and the villagers drag down dead timber from the woods, sawing it up in their back gardens. The woods belong to the Holnicote estate, and periodically, when the trees are thinned out, the villagers are allowed to take away the timber of felled trees for their fires. Wood-gathering on Sundays is still generally considered wrong, though other forms of light work such as washing are carried on frequently.

The cottages in Luccombe are fitted with coal-ranges by the Holnicote estate; and no open fireplaces are in use for cooking; the ranges are supplemented by paraffin and methylated-spirit stoves. The lack of gas is not felt seriously by housewives who have never used it, and though Calor gas in cylinders has long been available in country districts, so far as could be ascertained, the nearest Calor stove is at Horner. Mrs Prescott, who does all her cooking and heats her water on the range, says she would like to have Calor gas now; before the war she used to use three to four hundredweights of coal a week, but now she is only able to get one, and finds some difficulty in making do. It seems likely that the demand for Calor is accentuated, if not entirely caused, by wartime factors; otherwise one would have expected the villagers to have obtained it before.

There are baths in the two new council cottages, with cold taps and drains. Mrs Howard uses hers for the children, who have a weekly tub from water heated in the copper. The next-door bath is not used, as there are only kettles for water heating. One villager has a bath in her kitchen, but without outlet and not used; another has a hip-bath, which is not used either. None of the cottages has a water-heating system, and so far as can be ascertained it is the usual and perhaps universal practice in the village to have a stripwash in a basin.

Entrance Hall, Rose Cottage.

Living-room, Rose Cottage.

Bedroom, Rose Cottage.

Eight

HEALTH

THE usual basic first-aid remedies and materials are stocked at the village shop – boracic lint, cotton-wool, boracic ointment, vaseline, cough-mixture, liver pills, stomach- and indigestion-powder, and other simple remedies. Mrs Harold Prescott is a member of the St John's Ambulance Brigade and the only trained first-aid person in the village, and for minor injuries the villagers rely mainly on her, since the district nurse lives at Timberscombe and is only on the telephone before 9A.M. Mrs Strong, who till recently lived only a short way out of the village, at Luccombe Mill Farm, is a trained midwife and dealt with private maternity cases. For more serious ailments, a doctor has to be called in, but there is none nearer than Porlock or Minehead,. so most of the villagers die or are cured before the doctor arrives! Many of the villagers have one of the two Porlock doctors. Hospital cases normally go to Minehead, except for serious operations, which are done at Exeter.

The attitude of the villagers to health does not differ in any significant way from that of the townsman. Luccombe has abandoned the ancient folk-remedies and country superstitions for those of the modern city. A tin of liver salt has replaced the herbal tea – exactly what one would expect in a village which maintains regular contact with a town world. Faith in hopsitals is strong, but in doctors personal and variable. Yet in general doctors are accepted here in much the same way as anywhere else in contemporary England. There was an epidemic of influenza in the village a year or two ago. No one thought of calling in a doctor for this, at a guinea a visit, which is a normal charge for a call from Porlock – but no folk-remedies were in evidence either. People starved for a day, took tablets, magnesia, nothing more.

Bottles of medicine, made by a chemist at Minehead and prescribed by the doctor, are used for persistent illnesses among the children. Luccombe, in fact, treats its health like any modern community, turning to branded remedies when the illness is a minor one, to the district nurse when something more is needed, and to the doctor when it is serious.

There is no main drainage in Luccombe, and only a very small proportion of the houses have flush lavatories. The two council cottages in Stony Street have them, and these drain into a soak-away cess pool in Mr Staddon's meadow farther down the hill. All the other houses in this street have earth-closets, and the usual practice with this type of lavatory is to use a bucket of cinders. Household waste from some of the cottages drains into the stream which runs beside the road.

Nine
DOMESTIC LIFE

LUCCOMBE is not an example of strong village tradition. The inhabitants have often come from neighbouring parts within fairly recent years and their roots are in the county rather than in the narrower community. Communication with the outside world is relatively simple; most people get outside the village at regular intervals, and letting rooms also helps to keep Luccombe people in regular touch with people from other parts of the country. There is nothing peculiar to Luccombe about this picture: it could doubtless be repeated, with a change of names and a slight alteration of details, in any small agricultural village in England.

Old Mr Gould is the person the casual visitor to Luccombe is most likely to notice. He is over eighty and was born on November 18, 1866, in Devon; in 1891 he joined the police force. Exactly when he came to Luccombe is a little vague, but he came originally as a boy to help with horses:

> Of course, what I really like is the horses, anything to do with horses – horse fairs. You don't get them much now. Time was when we had horses all round. I like anything to do with horses... Ay, and there be some good hunts here. Many's the time I've been over Wheddon Cross for the meet. It's a fine sight. No, I don't ride, but mind I was allus in horses, like.

It would be easy to report many conversations of this kind and to turn Luccombe people into stock village types, but in this book the reader may see the villagers sufficiently portrayed in detail in the photographs.

The village community has its minor tension points, its family squabbles, its favourites and its buffoons, its social characters and its less social characters, like any other community. Mrs Blackmore, who lives a short way outside the village, has been there for nineteen years, and says she is not even yet accepted. But no one actually inside the village community is seriously unpopular with its members. The local 'gentry' and the inhabitants of the rectory evoke feelings ranging from tolerance to more positive liking and respect, but none of them has a very active contact with the community. Fitting in nowhere in the general pattern are the two old ladies, Misses Horn and Channen, who built a house just outside Luccombe nearly twenty years ago, and settled down to retire there. Mrs Keal – who lives by the lych-gate, was church cleaner for over twenty years before her amputation, and responsible for the church linen, which she laundered herself at Allerford laundry – says that, after all, they are only "strangers". 'Strangers' is the general name for those who have not been in the village long enough to be accepted as part of it, as well as for people from other parts who pass through it.

To be a good housewife and not to seek outside pleasures which will interfere with household duties is the general pattern of Luccombe respectability after marriage. Before marriage there seems to be a large measure of freedom between the sexes, as in most other communities, today. Little importance attaches to the rumour that few marriages have taken place before it was necessary, and no factual data is obtainable on this subject, the evidence being hearsay and gossip. Many rumours circulate in the village about the morals of others. It is of interest to note that they mostly concern those about whom the villagers in fact know least. Most rumours are simply the basis for gossip, and the general attitude is to hope for some development of the alleged situation rather than to condemn the people concerned, and there is always a decided interest in other people's morals. Luccombe, in fact, is typical of a small community in its excessive interest in 'knowing' about other people's lives.

China dresser, Rose Cottage

A corner of the kitchen, Rose Cottage

The landing, Rose Cottage

Ten
POLITICS

SINCE February 1944 the Holnicote estate, in which Luccombe stands, has belonged to the National Trust. Previously it was part of Sir Richard Acland's estate, and of Sir Thomas before him. This transfer seems to have made remarkably little impression on Luccombe people. They know very little about Sir Richard, and say he seldom visited the estate. "Isn't he a Liberal or something?" one of the women asked.

Sir Thomas Acland was much loved and respected and took an active interest in the welfare of his tenants, but there is small interest in Sir Richard. People have seen little or nothing of him, and reserve their judgment. The Common Wealth Party, of which he was the founder, arouses little interest either. There is an underlying scepticism, and little active interest in politics, outside election time, in Luccombe. Perhaps the impressions of one villager are worth quoting:

They have their committee rooms at Porlock. But I've known M.P.'s come down here and talk to the people. Ay, they take notice of us then, but it's the only time they do. But I wouldn't go if they didn't come and fetch me. I'm not interested in politics. Well, I don't know anything about it. I mean, you don't know who you're voting for, do you? You don't know whether you're doing the right thing. Some people in the village take a great interest, but myself – mind you, I think you ought to vote for an experienced man – me, I change around. I vote sometimes one way and sometimes the other. I think you need an experienced man. Like the one we've got now. I believe he's a very good man. Vernon Bartlett—that's who it is, isn't it, for round here? He's been all round the world, so, I mean, he's had the experience, you see. But I'm not the one to meddle with politics like some of them in the village. I was saying, only the other day, "There's more bad feeling and more friendships broken through politics than through any other thing."

The one Labour villager reads the Herald and talks vigorously and dogmatically against the 'gentry', but he is an exception. More typical is this remark about a visitor who once stayed in the village:

He was Socialist, you know. Not the sort of man I'd like to be seed out with. You'd soon get into a barny, you know. He'd got no time for gentry nor the likes o' they. I mind well the day I went out with him to buy some cigarettes. He was running down the farmers all the time, and I was very glad to get back indoors. No, I don't say you'll find any Socialists among the farmworkers here.

In general it would be true to say that the people of Luccombe are more impressed by personalities than politics. Class antagonism in this community is rare; such antagonisms as there are are personal, not general. Perhaps it was different in the old days, for Mr Gould, when asked if he argued about politics, replied: "I used to like it when I was a lad. Ay, there used to be some scenes down there in the pub; they used to get right wild about it, and many's the time I've been in a fight about it."

"Don't you get that now?"

"Oh, no; the beer's not strong enough now."

Eleven
THE DAILY ROUTINE

DURING the week Luccombe people get up early and go to bed early. The men have to get to work by seven o'clock, and six is a usual time for rising. Going to bed varies with the time of year; the men work in the gardens till dusk. But the village is usually quiet by nine, and ten o'clock is quite a usual time to be in bed. There are exceptions. Mrs Prescott, Miss Sims, and Mr Partridge stay up later, and Mrs Howard is often working well into the night.

Mr and Mrs Tame's daily routine is fairly typical. Mr Tame is a carter; and is about fifty-five years old. He has worked all his life at Blackford farm, starting at the age of ten. He and his wife get up soon after 6am each morning. They don't set an alarm-clock because Mrs Tame says, "You get used to the things, and they don't wake you", so they just rely on waking and always seem to manage it, however tired they are. Mrs Tame heats water and cooks breakfast with the aid of a primus and a methylated-spirit stove. Mr Tame goes to work on his bicycle, getting there at 7am, and his first job on arrival is to feed his three horses. "They knows when I'm coming, and as soon as I lay my bike against the wall they start neighing. They won't neigh for anyone else. 'Tis only my step they take notice of." After feeding and mucking out the horses he sits down to eat his own breakfast, which he carries with him in the form of sandwiches and a quart-sized bottle of tea. The tea will still be hot for the breakfast drink, but by midday it will be cold. However, Mr Tame does not mind and prefers to drink his tea cold than to have it in a thermos. But Mrs Tame makes use of a thermos. Last thing at night there is always plenty of water boiling on the hob, so she fills up her two large thermos flasks, and in the morning the water only takes a minute to boil up again for the first pot of tea.

After his breakfast, Mr Tame has many different jobs to do, according to the season and the weather. At about 12.30pm he knocks off for an hour and has his lunch. He finishes his jobs in the field between 5 and 5.30, and then he feeds and beds his horses down for the night. He arrives back at Porch Cottage about 6.30pm to find Mrs Tame putting the finishing touches to a two-course evening meal; so he takes off his jacket, rolls up his sleeves, turns in the neck of his shirt and has a good wash and shave. They then have supper – stewed steak and onions, potatoes, cauliflower, and rhubarb tart, on a typical evening. Water is drunk with the meal, and later on, about 9.30pm, they both have a cup of Bovril before going to bed. After supper Mr Tame goes straight out into his garden, for there is always plenty to do there.

This routine scarcely ever varies from day to day, except in the summertime, when he may be working overtime and may not get home until much later. On Saturdays he gets home about 1.30pm, so they have a hot meal at 2pm, and Mr Tame is busy in his garden for the rest of the day.

On Sundays the Tames do not get up so early. Breakfast is about 8.30am, after which the horses have to be fed, then back home to change into his best clothes to ring the church bells. He doesn't stay to the service, but comes home after ringing the bells. Until dinner time there may be odd jobs to do about the house, the Sunday papers to read; or he may pull out a few weeds, but he doesn't reckon to do any real gardening on a Sunday. After dinner he and his wife will sit a while and talk, and then perhaps take a walk up over the hill to see if there are any deer about or to look for some antlers.

Mrs Tame's day starts soon after 6am each week-day, when she gets up to prepare breakfast for her husband, who has to leave for his work about 6.45am. Between his departure and 10am Mrs Tame is very busy with her own housework. Between 10 and 10.30 she walks over to Wychanger, where she works until 3.30 for her old mistress, Mrs Lawrence. Mrs Tame has her dinner at Wychanger, and during the dinner hour usually does a little knitting. The only kind of knitting which she ever does is to make bedjackets, as she pretends she is too stupid to knit anything else. These garments are extremely well made and very effective; Mrs Tame has made quite a number and given them away to different people who happen to have admired them. "I can't keep anything", she says. "I give everything away."

Mrs Tame leaves Wychanger about 3.30 and walks slowly back to Porch Cottage, calling frequently at the Miss Palmers' house for a gossip. On arriving home she may make a cup of tea, but has no real meal until her husband returns between 6 and 6.30pm. Her afternoon is taken up with washing, ironing, housework – in fact, whatever needs doing – and of course the preparation and cooking of the evening meal.

After the meal comes washing up and the cutting of sandwiches for Mr Tame to take to work the following day. He likes cheese, supplemented by one or two of his wife's jam tarts or cakes, for Mrs Tame is an excellent cook, though she professes absolutely to hate it. By the time she has cleared away and packed up sandwiches ready for the next day it is getting on well into the evening, and she either goes out to watch her husband gardening and to have a chat with him, or goes round to Mrs Prescott to have a talk, invariably prefacing her remarks with, "Now, what do you think!"

As the evening draws in Mr Tame comes in from the garden and sits down in his armchair beside the range. He may idly glance through the paper if there is one about, or just sit still and rest while Mrs Tame makes a cup of Bovril, before they go to bed about 10pm.

Twelve
LEISURE

SUNDAY remains the day of rest in Luccombe. Best clothes are worn, although frequently people do not go beyond their house and garden or the village street. There is, however, little feeling that work should not be done on Sundays. Washing is often done by the women; the men, in wartime especially, sometimes have to work on the land. But Sunday is the day when people take things easy, get up late, keep indoors or in the garden in the morning, and walk or gossip in the village street in the late afternoon or evening. Here is an eyewitness account of a typical Luccombe Sunday scene:

The village has been extremely quiet all day. No one was about at 9am. At 10am there were signs of life in the houses, but no one in the streets. The church service on the B.B.C. could be heard from Mrs Tame II's house, and from Mrs Keal's. Mrs Keal says she always listens, as she can't go to church because of her leg.

The villagers – that is, the general part of the village – did not go to church. Apart from children, only Mrs Tame II and the two Miss Palmers represented this section at church. Nevertheless, on leaving church, one met no one in the street. Even Mrs Gould wasn't on her step. Mrs Wylde was hanging out her washing; Mr Hale was fixing up a deckchair in the back garden; Nancy Sully stood at her doorway; Mrs Webber had done quite a lot of washing.

In the afternoon most of the men sat in their arm-chairs and had a sleep. At 2.30pm Mr Wylde was standing in his Sunday best gazing contemplatively at his vegetable garden. Mrs Webber was standing in a flowered apron at her side door; two or three children were playing along the road; Tony Hale and his girlfriend Queenie were walking along the lane.

From Knowle Top it could be seen that several families were sitting in their gardens in deckchairs – the Rowlands, Hales, and others.

A few people came out in the evening. At 6pm several men were gathered at the Keals' doorstep. At 6.30pm there was another church service. All the evening the two Arscott girls sat on their steps with the Italian prisoners of war, whistling at passers-by. Young boys on bicycles cycled aimlessly up and down. One of the Arscotts in partic-ular was executing a cycling trick – cycling backwards in circles.

Mr Howard and Mr Webber went to a Wootton Courtney pub in the evening. At 7.30pm Mrs Amber was chatting with Mrs Gande outside the Gandes' house. Miss Coles, cloth cap on head, was working in her garden. Arscotts as before.

At 9pm there was no one down the street. At the corner by the shop, Mr Keal, in his Sunday suit with a grey alpaca jacket instead of his brown one, was standing talking to the policeman, who is in the wartime auxiliary police and is really a farmer from Horner. Nancy Sully, in a flowery green dress, stood at the Keals' door with Winifred Sully in her white flannel night-gown.

At 9.30pm Tony Hales cycled back from a visit to Queenie. Mr Staddon, in Sunday clothes – blue jacket, grey trousers, cloth cap –

walked out from his house followed by his collie-dog. He went over
to his dairy to look at the cows. Mrs Rowland, in a pink flowered
overall, went into the Staddon house. Mr Keal went indoors. Mr
Moore stood outside his house playing with the children; Basil
Howard was playing in his front garden.

That is Luccombe on a Sunday, resting and moving around slowly and
locally. How Luccombe spends its spare time through the week and
through the year, what its interests and its fulfilments are, we shall now
see.

All the village cottages, except Mr Partridge's, the Webbers', and the
Wyldes', have a wireless-set. The Webbers have been unable to get one;
the Wyldes and Mr Partridge don't want one. All but four of the cottages
take a daily paper, and all but three a Sunday paper. The ones who don't
take a daily paper say they haven't time to read it, except for Mrs Wylde,
who says she never bothers. Mrs Rowland adds: "We don't take a daily
paper because it doesn't come until after we've heard the news on the
wireless, and no one has time to read it."
The national newspapers read are:

Daily Mail	six
Daily Express	six
News Chronicle	four
Daily Mirror	two
Daily Herald	two

No one reads *The Times, Telegraph,* or *Daily Graphic.* Many households
take two Sunday papers. Of the thirty-two which are read in the twenty-
one cottages that take them, ten are unspecified. These are the people
who vary their Sunday reading, or take whatever is available. The papers
taken on Sunday are:

News of the World	nine
People	five
Sunday Pictorial	five
Sunday Express	one
Sunday Graphic	one
Sunday Dispatch	one
Unspecified	ten

Apparently Miss Sims and the Blackmores are the only households
which do not read the *West Somerset Free Press* once a week. This paper
contains the local news, parish by parish, in great detail. At the time of
the death of the Howard boy, for instance, details of the inscriptions on
every one of the numerous wreaths sent was included in the report. All
the villagers whose roots are in Luccombe read it.
The following periodicals are also taken in the village:

Radio Times	three
Picture Post	two
John Bull	two
Farmer and Stockbreeder	two
Home Notes	one
Sunday Companion	one

This list of periodicals, compiled from information supplied by representatives of each household, is possibly not complete, since it is easy to
overlook a weekly or monthly paper taken by some other member of the

family. But this information is enough to show that a wide range of daily and periodical literature reaches the cottagers. The entire absence of the so-called 'quality' papers is not surprising, but is worth noting. *The Times, Telegraph, Observer, Sunday Times,* and more serious periodicals are not taken. Luccombe people keep in touch with the news through the mass-circulation papers and the B.B.C. Nearly every one has a daily and a Sunday paper, and nearly every one a radio. In this respect Luccombe is no more isolated than any urban community, and its tastes do not differ in any significant respect from those of people with similar incomes in a town.

Not many books are read in Luccombe: people have too much to do out of doors and are too busy with their housework and odd jobs; then they go to bed very early. One bookcase we saw contained a Bible and a Prayer Book, a selection of miscellaneous novels, gardening books, and books of local interest, stretching over a long period, with a slight scattering of volumes of more recent date. (Contents of two typical bookshelves from two of the cottages are given in Appendix I.) Nancy Sully, who has nothing to do, except to help her grandmother with her housework, is one of the few who do a good deal of reading, but as one might expect it is mostly 'shockers'.

There are hunting books in some of the cottages. In general Luccombe book reading is occasional and light. In contrast, Mrs Keal has a copy of *Memories of a Stag Harbourer,* by Fred Goss (for many years harbourer to the Devon and Somerset Staghounds), of which she is very proud. The county provides a quarterly library service, and the books are delivered to Miss Sims, who is responsible for their distribution. This service is used by very few of the villagers, and those who do read do so mostly in the winter. The books are predominantly light novels and travel stories. The Staddons, Rowlands, Mr Partridge, and Miss Sims are the chief readers.

Thirteen
TOWN DIVERSIONS

FROM what has been said about the women's varied occupations it might be supposed that they had little time for anything but their own and other people's housework. In fact, it is the women far more than the men who get outside the village. Luccombe is the meeting-place of four roads; to the north-west is Porlock, to the north-east Minehead, to the south-east Wootton Courtney, to the south-west Exford. Both Porlock and Minehead are equally accessible by bus from Brackley Steps, one-and-a-quarter miles from the village. Even in wartime ten buses a day passed in each direction.

Apart from holidays, Minehead is practically the only place to which Luccombe women go; a few of them never seem to leave the village at all. Although Porlock is nearer and equally accessible, they prefer Minehead because it is a bigger shopping centre and affords more of a contrast to the seclusion of Luccombe. Visits to Minehead are frequent. Some go once or twice a week, others go about once a month, a few go only occasionally. Miss Sims, who comes from Staffordshire, falls outside the general pattern and explains, "I never go outside the village except when I go home for my holidays. There's nowhere to go. Minehead certainly isn't worth going to."

Most of those who visit Minehead frequently are the younger people. The older women tend to go less often, and for the very old and ailing the walk to the bus is a practical deterrent. Several of the older ones, however, hire a car regularly to take them from the village, clubbing together to pay the cost and making a day of it. Before the war Mr Prescott, the haulier, ran a hire-car; it had to be laid up because of petrol restrictions. But the practice still carried on, cars being hired from Minehead at eight shillings to ten and sixpence the single journey. For most of these women the visit to Minehead is a shopping expedition primarily; as Mrs Wylde said, "I don't go much to the pictures. They tries my eyes, and I think us country folk think more about what we can buy to eat than going for pleasure."

The men visit Minehead rarely; and among the older generation of both sexes picture-going is often a faint memory. Mrs French has been twice in six years; Mrs Howard goes about twice a year; Mr Hales has never been in his life and old Mr Gould's last visit dates back to some time early in the silent-film days. Nevertheless, there is a good deal of picture-going and some dancing among the few remaining representatives of the younger generation, and even one or two of the older ones go to the cinema regularly. Mrs Fred Blackmore, for instance, says she usually goes to the pictures on Wednesdays, after her weekly visit to the insurance office for which she is an agent.

One of the young women said to us, "I go to Minehead once or twice a week to the pictures, or dances at the Regal. There used to be dances at Porlock, but they're no good now. They've only got a radiogram. Sometimes they have dances at Wootton, but not now the summer's come." Jimmy Shopland and Mervyn Arscott go regularly each Saturday to Minehead together. Mervyn plays the drums in a local band and is out with it once or twice a week; Jimmy does not play, but goes with Mervyn.

There are so few youngsters in the village today that it is impossible to generalize. But judging by those there are, it would appear that the new generation of Luccombe people are little affected by the physical remoteness of the village in their choice of amusements. On the other hand, Nancy Sully, asked if she went out much, replied, "No, only into the street", and painted a gloomy picture of herself sitting at home knitting.

There used at one time to be weekly dances in the Luccombe parish hall, but the demand was not strong enough, and they were reduced to once a fortnight and finally dropped altogether.

But though the women and young people of Luccombe like to get outside the village into a new environment from time to time, this does not imply any dissatisfaction with village life. Mrs Prescott, after returning from a visit to Bristol said:

Oh, my word I don't know how people can stick living in a town. It seems so dirty, and the people look so shabby. I don't know, but I get a funny feeling when I walk down the street that people are looking at me and saying "she doesn't come from here". I feel sort of cleaner than they are. I think people in towns wear shabby clothes. They may be a bit smart, but it's gaudy, and it's not good. I couldn't buy cheap stuff like that. And, oh – the dirt! I was noticing Mrs C's windows. You can't leave the windows up for long or all the dirt comes in... I was looking at her larder. She's got a glass door, I shouldn't mind some of her tins of fruit. Still, we're better off in the country. We can get some decent fresh vegetables and things out of our garden...

If you ask Luccombe people what they think of country life or how they occupy themselves without city distractions they are frankly puzzled. But naturally although Luccombe is a beauty-spot and a holiday place, Luccombe people themselves like to go elsewhere for their own holidays. Mrs Amber, for instance, goes to her sister in Dorchester; the Prescotts go to Wokingham; the Howards go to Dulverton; the old Tames went to the Isle of Wight two years ago, their first holiday for twenty years; the Misses Palmer go away every year to different places; Miss Coles goes to London and Warwickshire; the young Mr and Mrs Tame go to Surrey; Nora Arscott goes away regularly to different places – Bristol, Shrewsbury, and this year, she hopes, Oswestry; Mrs Blackmore went to London recently and was hoping to get to Newcastle in the summer, though her husband stays behind because he doesn't like visiting; and Miss Sims goes home to Staffordshire. Mrs French farmed in Canada for seven years; young Mrs Tame had been twice to Switzerland with her mistress before she was married; the Rev Howard was a missionary in Australia. And so, between them, the villagers have a fair experience of other parts of the world.

Fourteen
COUNTRY DIVERSIONS

AT Exford the famous Devon and Somerset Staghounds are kennelled. There are hacking stables at the Dunkery Hotel, Wootton Courtney, and several at Porlock. Most famous are Collins's; they breed, break, make, and deal in horses, and the Collins family have been noted for horsemanship for many generations. The present owner, Mr Tony Collins, married a famous horsewoman, Josephine Colebrook. Normally two hundred horses are kept there.

For the people of Exmoor, horses and hunting, stags and foxes, form a common topic of conversation. Anyone connected with farming automatically becomes an honorary member of the hunt, and can enjoy the sport for nothing. It is not unusual to see a farm labourer strip the gear off his working horse, jump on its back, and plod along with the rest of the field for a mile or two. In Porlock some of the local shops close down on the day of the meet, and the tradesman goes off for the day with the hunt. Many who do not ride follow on foot.

For Luccombe villagers, hunting is largely a matter of attending the meet and, perhaps, following on foot; or running out from their houses to watch the hunt pass. "Ay, it be a rare sight", is the general response to an inquiry about hunting. One of the village women told us the story of a hunting accident which lingers in her memory in vivid detail:

> I had some visitors once, and they were mad keen to see some hunting. It was a pouring wet day. The rain was absolutely teeming down – just as it does sometimes – only this day was much worse than I can ever remember it raining. Well, these two ladies were sitting indoors when all of a sudden I said, "Hark, I can hear the horn. They're quite near, coming down the Coombe. If you like I'll come out with you and see if we can see them." Presently Mr Forster came galloping up and said, "Have you seen which way they've gone, Mrs Tame?" "I think they've gone up to Horner", I said. So he said: "I think I'll go up over to Webber's Post and down the Coombe."
> Well, we stood there waiting, not minding the rain a bit, but they didn't come back, so we went on home. Presently the baker came from Porlock. He said to me: "Mr Forster's gone." I said: "Yes, I know."
> "Dead, I mean," he said. "Don't be silly," I said, "I've just been talking to him not half an hour ago. He said he would ride down Horner Water." "Well, he's dead, anyway. His body has just been recovered on Bossington beach with all his clothes washed off." Well, I couldn't believe it, but it was quite right, for my husband was down at Allerford shoeing when Doctor Tatlow came along and shouted for men to go and stand at the bridges and watch for a body. Dreadful thing it was, dreadful, and he was so young. And the funny thing was, his horse was dry under the saddle. They never did know what happened, for no one was with him at the time. He might have had a stroke or something crossing the stream. His horse wasn't hurt at all. What a dreadful thing to have to go and tell his poor wife. A nice gentleman he was too. I must have been one of the last to speak to him.

In peacetime there is an opening meet of the Staghounds at Cloutsham Ball during August. Bank Holiday is not kept on the farms, but the day of the meet is a general holiday, and men, women, and children turn out in their hundreds to watch. Tea and refreshments are served to all comers at Cloutsham farm.

An exception to the general interest in hunting is Mr Staddon's attitude; he farms the glebe land in Luccombe with his brother, and he confesses that if he had his time over again he wouldn't be a farmer and that he has more sympathy with the shooting than the hunting of foxes. But for the most part hunting is in the villagers' blood, and the sight of the hunt, or a glimpse of a stag is an event to talk over. The children often go up to the meet and follow on their own. Winifred Sully, aged eight, told us how she and her sister were in at the kill after the meet at Webber's Post:

I shall always remember the day we went hunting up at Webber's Post. Me and Nancy went together. It was ever such fun. Hounds were on to two young stags, so they divided and some went one way and some t'other. We ran after them. It was ever so exciting. We went miles. It was fun, and they killed the deer, and we had some liver. I like liver. Don't you? Nancy, she don't like it. It's nice fried in the pan with a bit of bacon. And venison – that's nice too.

And she told us of a private stag hunt by the children:

One day we were picking up lightings in the wood here when a girt great stag jumped up from behind a tree. He gave us such a fright. He'd been lying down, and we didn't notice him until he jumped up. We did have some fun. There were several of us and we played at hunting. We chased him miles through the woods. I hit him with one of my sticks.

Jimmy Shopland and his father, and Mr Partridge are the only Luccombe villagers who are likely to be seen mounted at a meet, Jimmy on a pony borrowed from Mr Spence Thomas, of Huntscote, Mr Shopland on his working horse. Mr Partridge takes the day off for a meet regularly in peacetime. He also walked hound puppies, whose mischievous activities are still a topic of conversation in the village.

I had one [said Mr Partridge] used to go off into Minehead by himself – regular nuisance he was. Many's the time I've had to take an' ride the pony in arter him. Once I had to buy a shilling's worth of cakes to entice he home. One of them had a trick of carrying things off. Take anything he would. At the time they were building this house on the hills it was. The workmen up there were all keen stag hunters and used to make a fuss of the puppy. They used to bring field-glasses to watch the deer on the hill opposite. Well, one day they put the glasses down, and the next thing was the blinking hound was off down the road with these blinking glasses. The fellow said he never would have believed it if he hadn't seen it with his own eyes.

Trophies of the hunt, mounted 'slots', stags' antlers, and bundles of stag's hair adorn the cottage walls. Also, in some of the cottages, are foxes' masks. Mr Hales, gardener up at Wootton Courtney, who is very keen on hunting, has an intimate knowledge of horses, and worked over in Ireland as a groom in his younger days, keeps a fox's mask over the lintel of his front door, a slot on the door, and a horseshoe as a knocker. The Goulds, the Ambers, and the Rowlands have brass knockers in the form of a stag's head. Almost every house and cottage in Luccombe contains some evidence of the people's love of hunting – antlers, masks, brushes, stags' hair, and pads are displayed on the walls of the hall or the living-room. Out of twenty-four houses about twenty contain trophies.

The slots are the stags' feet, distributed after the hunt; and the hair is pulled from the animal after the kill. Stags' antlers are picked up in the surrounding woods and fields in the spring when the animals shed them. It is rare to find a pair, since they are not often shed at the same time, and a perfect pair of antlers is a treasured possession. A perfect antler consists of bow, bey, trey, and two or more atop. This is to say, a central beam with three main offshoots, and two or more small offshoots at the top.

Mr Howard has a stag's antler, which he says is almost perfect, but the trey is missing. He says:

> If I had two of he t'would be what they call a double-crown. I could get four pounds for they, if I had the other. You'd never believe it only took a year to grow he; ay, they shed they every year, and it takes a year to grow a new one. Like now, you might see they with a little bit of horn, and by the end of the year he'll have grown he full.
> Strong too. You'd never believe the strength in he. I got it up on Dunkery. The children were going for a walk, and they sat down, and they were sitting on he. I've got some slots too; they be mounted proper with the name and date and when he were killed.

Another Luccombe sporting interest is otter hunting, and Mr Howard went on:

> Ay, hunting's a grand sight. I'm not very good on the hunt, though. I don't care for riding and the hunt. Unless it be otter hunting. Oh, ay, I been otter hunting many a time. Otter hunting is done on foot. You can sell the furs – like foxes. Some years back I set rabbit snares all round the field, and I miss some of the rabbits in the morning. So I say nothing; but next night I set a rabbit at the top of an earth and the gin right by it. The next morning there's a beauty of a fox caught in 'un. I get he proper. I have to go carefully. They be like wild dogs, they foxes. I gets a big stick and hits he over the head, and tie up the legs, and in my bag he goes. (For I always carry a bag, as they say.) So I take he along to Mr Partridge; but he aren't in. But the house-keeper, she say, "Put he into the shed till Mr Partridge come home." So I puts the bag into the shed and locks the door. When Mr Partridge comes home the housekeeper say, "There's a surprise for ye in the shed," and Mr Partridge he go into the shed, and that old fox, the s bitten through the string and got loose. But Mr Partridge kills he. And the fur – Mrs Prescott got that afore she were married.

Tools used at Ley Farm

Carts in the farmyard at Ley Farm

Corn is still threshed by hand against this barrel at Ley Farm

Ring roller in use at Ley Farm

Horse harrow or horse hoe in use at Ley Farm

Sheep-dipping at Horner Water

Fifteen

PETS

APART from the livestock on the farms, the working horses, the hunters and hacks, the deer and the foxes and the rabbits, Luccombe is a village of animals. The children have pet rabbits; there are eleven dogs in the village; two ponies; one donkey; one nannie-goat and one canary. Three of the dogs – Sport, Jimmy Shopland's, Guard, Mr Staddon's sheepdog, Rosie, one of Mr Partridge's two sheep-dogs – are continually about the village and are known and fondled by the children. The four working sheepdogs do not go far from their masters, but Sport regularly accompanies the children on their walks.

The goat is chiefly in evidence. Tony Hales bought it for his friend Queenie, who was at Holt Ball Farm, but either she couldn't keep it or she didn't want it, so Tony keeps it on a long chain on the village green. Walking past the green, you can often see Mr Shopland, Jimmy Shopland, and Tony Hales standing opposite the telephone-box watching the goat on the other side of the road eating nettles and nibbling branches.

MR SHOPLAND: They'd eat anything.

JIMMY: They don't eat it. They just nibble.

MR SHOPLAND: I don't know. He made short work of one of my leather gaiters the other day.

[They watch the goat. A herd of cattle go round the bend about twenty-five yards down the road.]

MR SHOPLAND: They be fine bullocks.

TONY: Ay. That they be.

[A man on a horse trots through the cows, and instead of turning the bend with them, comes towards the group. Two dogs race after him. He shouts out something about the bullocks as he passes.]

MR SHOPLAND: That be Mr Williams on the farm. He be going to get cigarettes from the shop that's where he be going.

JIMMY: I've seen him riding fast as anything on the hardest of the camber.

TONY: Ay, he be a fast rider, Mr Williams.

JIMMY: They dogs, they be good sheepdogs.

TONY: Ay, silent them be, and no barking, but they do hold the sheep in a straight line in the field.

[Back comes Mr Williams, and again shouts something as he passes. They watch the goat. Jimmy picks up a rabbit gin and begins fiddling with it. He reads the trademark "Li-Lo".]

TONY: Ay, and they do lie low till the rabbit do tread on 'un.

MR SHOPLAND: They be good traps. Now then, Jimmy, 'tis the wrong way to hold 'un.

JIMMY Ay, this be the right way.

[He demonstrates. Tony goes over to the goat and fondles it. He cuts a branch from a bush, and comes back whistling and whittling it. He shapes it like the rest of the stakes, selects an old stake to throw away, and replaces it with the new one.]

The villagers' thoughts run on animals – hunting animals, shooting animals, looking after animals, pet animals, animals to eat, animals to tend, animals to love. Old Mrs. Keal, asked what she said when she came round from the anaesthetic after her amputation, replied:

> Oh, I was very quiet. Very quiet, they said. Only that was in the war, and he [her husband] was away, and I was looking after fifteen bullocks, and all I could think of was worrying whether they were feeding them. I kept saying I wondered whether they'd been fed all right. They say the last thing you think of before you go off is the thing you talk about, don't they? Though I don't remember thinking that. I don't remember thinking anything. I was too tired.

Sixteen
GARDENS, PUBS AND SMALL TALK

THERE is no inn in Luccombe, nor anywhere on the Acland Estate. The nearest is at Wootton Courtney. There is virtually no social centre in Luccombe beyond the doorstep and the village street. The parish hall, which was presented to the village shortly after the First World War and is an old army hut, is rarely used now. Today, beyond an occasional whist drive, a rare meeting of the parish council, and the quarterly attendance of the villagers to pay their rent, the hall is generally kept locked.

Some of the men go fairly regularly to Wootton or Porlock inns at the weekend, but it is usually on a Saturday or Sunday – seldom both. Mr Gould remembers brown ale at threepence a pint, and says he used to go every evening, wet or fine, to Wootton. Today, on an old-age pension, his visits are rare. His son is a teetotaller, and Bill Tame is another.

Although Somerset is famous for its cyder, and home-brewed cyder is found at many small farms and drunk by young and old alike, Mr Partridge is the only Luccombe person who has it. Another farmer, Mr Staddon, prefers beer, though he seldom drinks it owing to lack of time for getting to the pub:

Now, cyder is something I can't abide. I like a drop of brown ale myself, the real thing. Beer's very good stuff, or should be. It's got all the best in it – hops and barley. And that's another thing – these parts round here are known for their barley. My barley crop all went to make beer this year, you know that. Ay, and over there there's a field won the prize for the whole country for barley last year. And one year, over in Porlock, they won the prize for the whole world. So there you are – if you're interested in drinking – there's the finest barley in the world in these parts.

A visit to Wootton Courtney on a Saturday evening might find three or four Luccombe men in the "Dunkery". The bar is part of a large and rather superior-looking hotel which is set back in a large garden up a gravel drive. It is a white building with a verandah. The public bar like most country bars is small, with two tables, two benches, and not enough chairs.

A visitor at about seven o'clock in the evening would find Bob Prescott, looking tired and weather-beaten, slumped up in a chair next to the bar; Mr Hales, who has cycled from Luccombe, sitting in a chair by the window; a man of forty-five not from Luccombe in the next-door chair; Mr Keal, who has walked in, standing leaning on his cane. Talk centres on horses. One or two more men come in and join in the talk. The Wootton baker in his brown overall and cloth cap is likely to come in and eventually the conversation will break up into groups. At 8pm Mr Prescott leaves; Mr Wylde arrives and sits in his seat. Ten men are present now, and conversation round the bar is about a stony field. "Ay, that's the stoniest one you got, George, bain't it?". . . "Big stones". . . "One along of Dunkery be stonier". . . "Proper hard". . . "Never see such big stones". . . "Stoniest I got."

The window group pick up the conversation and talk of stones in general. One man brings out a box of snuff, and offers it all round. Most men accept it. "Never say no to a pinch of snuff" . . . "Ay, I likes a bit of he." Mr Keal says he never touches it. A well-dressed man, chef to a local family, says he doesn't mind a bit, "but it be a right bad habit to get into". The old man in overalls says he never refuses a pinch but doesn't carry any around.

By nine o'clock the room is getting smoky. There are thirteen men present, three of them from Luccombe. The conversation runs on horses, root crops, personalities, the Porlock pub, the invasion, a story about a German airman, the Home Guard, and the chocolate ration.

At 9.15 two Americans enter. From then on the conversation, which is of farming all the time, is dominated by the Americans – by one, in particular, who was a farmer in America. At 10pm it is "Time, please," and the men finish off rather quickly, form in a small knot outside, and then, "fine-nighting" each other, set off on bicycles or on foot.

Few women from Luccombe ever go into a pub, and for the men it is only an occasional social evening. Of the young people, Mervyn Arscott drinks a little, and in the absence of other young men, he can be taken as a typical Luccombe youth. Mervyn is eighteen, a tallish, pink-faced, goodlooking lad, entirely unaffected. He wears much-patched grey flannels tucked into his boots, a scarf, a very high-necked jumper with a zip fastener, and a jacket. He drinks and smokes moderately. Miss Coles, of the village shop, says of him:

"He's a very moderate boy. Oh yes, he knows how to behave. Not like some. There's one boy comes in for a packet of twenty every day. Dreadful boy. Still, there's not many like that round here."

This is praise indeed, from Miss Coles. Mervyn has a rather quick temper, but he is gentle and very fond of animals. At a circus in Minehead recently he was upset that one of the ponies seemed terrified while taking part in a trick in which an elephant walked over him. He likes the pictures and goes regularly; but though he plays regularly in a dance band, he doesn't like dancing himself. One of the reasons why people don't go oftener to the pub is lack of money. Two hedgers and ditchers working on a ditch near the rectory – one an old man of about seventy from Horner, the other about thirty-five from Porlock – when asked what they did in the evenings, replied:

"There be plenty of work. Last night I didn't finish till gone ten. Then there be the lodgers, like, and doing teas and all."

"Don't you go out on a Saturday?"

"No, I be working come ten o'clock then."

"Well, when do you have time for a drop of beer?"

"I never have no time. Besides they don't give us the pay; there's none to pay for the likes of 'er."

"Who do you work for?"

"We be on the council."

"Don't you go out either?"

"No, not that much. They give un £6.8s.4d. a fortnight. It don't breach no goings out."

"Pictures?"

"I never been to pictures in my life."

But for the most part the men stay at home because they don't want to go anywhere else. They lean on the rail opposite Mr Webber's house, or gather in the Square, at the meeting of the roads, opposite the shop. And they work in their gardens.

Working in the garden is more than a hobby for the men. The cultivation of vegetables is an essential addition to the household economy. Mr Howard, who works in a market garden all day, returns home in the evening to work in his own. Gardening is not a 'change', a positive relaxation from different work, as it is for the town worker; it is a continuation, and, like farm work, it brings its own satisfaction. Mr Wylde, after a day on the roads, is working at 7.30 of a spring evening on his own large strip of vegetable garden.

"Working hard?"

"Ay, that I be. I grow all my own vegetables. I never don't buy no vegetables at all. You have to know what to plant. They were Brussel sprouts before, and now it be cabbage, and I be digging it up now for beans. They come one after the other, only you got to know what to plant. I never don't buy nothing in the shops. Ay, it's worth it. Mind you, it's a big patch! I was showing it to a gentleman and his wife the other night, and he was saying it was more like a field than a garden. But it's worth it. I never have to buy vegetables. It's not like town life, where the woman has to bring out money for every pound of potatoes she has. We grow all our own here."

When the available space is not large enough the villagers are often given land on the farms for their own use. They are not charged for the use of the land, but the farmer expects them to come and help him out with the harvesting later in the year, when he is short-handed.
Mrs Tame once explained this system:

> I thought Frank would be home this afternoon, but he went off back to the farm as soon as he'd had his dinner. He's potato-planting for the men. Mr Ridler lets them all have a piece of ground to plant their potatoes. They all help each other. Frank's driving the horses this afternoon and the others are coming behind and planting the potatoes. Perhaps next week they'll all go up to Mr Connelly's to help plant there. It's much easier and quicker that way when they all work together.
>
> Mr Connelly doesn't charge them anything for the ground, but when it comes harvesting time, and he needs extra men, he likes them to come and help then. So unless Frank is busy at Blackford, he goes down all he can. Mr Connelly doesn't expect them to do it for nothing, either. He pays them very well indeed. A real nice gentleman he is, and very understanding. If Frank's harvesting at Blackford of course he can't go, and Mr Connelly doesn't expect him to.

Through co-operation of this sort, and through the work the men put into their gardens, Luccombe manages to be self-supporting in vegetables. In normal times, too, Luccombe people do not have to go outside their own village for milk, cream, butter or eggs. The Staddons supply all the villagers but one with milk. In peacetime Mr Partridge used to pick up some five hundred eggs a day from his two thousand poultry, and many of the villagers keep hens themselves. Some also keep a pig in their garden, which they fatten for eating.

Seventeen
MARKETS

VISITS to the market on farming business take the farmers outside the village. When there is a beast for sale the farmer almost invariably attends personally, usually travelling down with the animals on the lorry. Here is an account of a visit to Taunton market.

One morning we went with Mr Strong, of Luccombe Mill, who had a store bullock for sale, and had arranged with a Minehead contractor to take it by lorry to Taunton market. He was dressed in dark-grey trousers, black waistcoat and jacket, white shirt with black pin-stripe, stiff white collar and black tie, grey socks, and black shoes. In the village he usually wore white plimsolls, flannel shirt, and old dark serge trousers and jacket. The lorry was due to arrive at the farm at 7.30am, and at 7.45am it turned up. Mervyn had been to work early and was waiting to help with the loading. Mr Strong was still indoors struggling into his best suit.

MERVYN: Morning.
DRIVER: Morning – that the bullock?
MERVYN: That's the one.
DRIVER: Nice young bullock.
MERVYN: Ah – I've been feeding thic. Didn't know as he was going till boss told me last night.
DRIVER: What's matter wid 'un?
MERVYN: A breaker.
DRIVER: That is it ——!
MERVYN: When thic bullock and a young heifer we've got get together there's no field'll hold 'em. Proper devils they be.
DRIVER: Um. Well, let's load 'un up.
[They start to let down tail-boards, but one lever catches on the corrugated-iron roof of the shed.]
MERVYN: Us can't move roof.
DRIVER: No – us'll have to move lorry.
[He gets in, moves the lorry, and lets down the back end; he goes inside the lorry and shakes up the straw on the floor. Both men then try to drive the bullock in, but it won't go.]
DRIVER: Just a moment. I've got it.
[He goes into the lorry, brings out a handful of straw and shakes it out on the runway. The bullock then walks up without any trouble.]
MERVYN: Well, I'm damned.
DRIVER: They don't like to hear the rattle of their hooves on the boards.
[The driver begins to fasten up the lorry.]
MERVYN: What about thic bag o' hay and they sacks?
DRIVER: What be they for?
MERVYN: Boss wants to take along some hay for 'un to eat in pen. He reckons her won't be sold till fairly late.
DRIVER: Her don't want that.
MERVYN: Us 'ud better put it in. Where be us going to put 'un?
DRIVER: 'Er won't hurt.

MERVYN: Her's just had a girt great armful of hay so I don't say 'er'll hurt, but better see boss. But they bags have got to go. Put 'em in along o' bullock. They won't hurt.

DRIVER: Morning, Mr Strong.

MR STRONG: Morning. I wanted to take along a bag of hay for the bullock to eat whilst it's standing.

DRIVER: How are you going to feed 'un if it is penned up along o' a lot of others? He won't hurt. Let 'un bide.

MR STRONG: Well, it could go in, and it could ride on top of the cab.

DRIVER: He's had a good meal. He won't hurt nothing.

MR STRONG: All right, Mervyn. Empty 'un out. I must have the sack to go back.

So we started on our twenty-five-mile journey, and as we passed through Luccombe about 8am not a soul was to be seen anywhere. We made only one call, to pick up a cow at a farm which keeps a pedigree herd of T.T. cows.

DRIVER [to cowman]: What you got this morning Jim – an old barrener?

JIM: Her's a reacter. Beautiful cow. Boss paid a hundred and fifty pounds for her only a few weeks ago, but she reacted, so we be bound to put her out. Pity – some one will have a cheap cow. There's no reserve on her. But I say if she's not good enough for us she shouldn't be good enough for anyone else's herd. But there you are, anyone can keep her if they haven't got a T.T. herd. Her milk's all right, no T.B. there. But she's got it in her. All cows have got T.B., but some are strong enough to resist the disease and don't react to the test. Her's got a nice calf. Bull calf. We be keeping that. She's got a pedigree as long as my arm.

Farmer Strong showed great interest and asked questions about the cow – how old, how much milk she gave, etc., and went into the dairy with the cowman to look at the records. We passed a very large herd of dairy cattle on the road, whereupon Mr Strong and the driver discussed the merits of different cows, and the driver in several cases was able to give a short life-history of the cow under discussion. This was rather amazing, but the driver explained: "You see a lot on my job. And you see a lot of dodges done. Especially among the horses. I smile to myself many times when I see them passing round."

When we got to Bagborough and Lydeard St Lawrence, Mr Strong took great pride in pointing out the house where he was born. The farm his father farmed, which his brothers now farm, and which he himself farmed before moving to Luccombe. He pointed out the house where J.C. White the cricketer lives and told us that Sir Dennis Boles built the house especially for him. It is a very plain modern house, and Mr Strong said, "Myself, I'd rather live in the old farmhouse. It is a nice old house, but that new one is very ugly."

We arrived at the market entrance about 10.15.

DRIVER [to girl in box]: Two cattle – cow and a steer.

GIRL: Two cattle —

DRIVER [to Mr Strong]: Sometimes if you just say "Two cattle" they say, "What do you mean, 'two cattle'?" And if you've got a cow with her own calf you say "Cow and calf", but if it isn't the cow's calf, you must say "one cow, one calf".

We drew into the market and prepared to unload. The market opened at

10am; it was then nearly 10.30, and we were among the first arrivals. We unloaded the cow first amid shouts of "Come on, sweetheart . . . quiet with 'er~now . . . this way sweetheart . . . look out, Miss . . . head 'er off . . . no yer don't . . . her wants 'er calf . . . come on, sweetheart. Always be quiet with a cow, Miss. Tell us, Miss, did 'er slip 'er calf? Her looks a nice cow. Did you see her calf?"

The auctioneer came up in his car, got out, and had a look. "Where did she come from? Um reacter, I suppose."

To which the driver replied, "Cowman says she's a very good cow – three and a half gallon a day."

We then proceeded to unload the steer and had much fun chasing it from pen to pen, as there appeared to be some confusion as to whether it was to be entered with the store cattle or graded. There were two men running round with pencils and forms. One was old and deaf, and the other young and full of fun. Eventually it was penned up, and by this time many other lorries were moving in, some with bags of hay on board. Mr Strong noticed this and remarked to us: "He could have brought some hay, you know. That bullock could have been feeding now. I'm so afraid her'll look pinched up by the time her's sold."

There was nothing to be done about it, so he said he'd be off to the other end of the town to take back some bags and have a cup of tea. By 11.15 Mr Strong was back in the market wandering around and waiting for the auctioneer to commence selling. He met Dick Willmets, a well-known dealer, and had a conversation with him regarding a cart-mare Dick bought very cheaply at a recent sale, and which Mr Strong would very much have liked to buy because he hoped to get it cheap. (It was known to have been bought by Dick for £6.5s., and Mr Strong hoped to buy it for eight or ten pounds, whereas it was probably worth all of twenty!) As is the way with dealers, Dick switched the conversation from horses to bullocks and offered to come over to Luccombe and do a deal.

By this time the auctioneer had started selling the cows and calves, and Mr Strong stood silently at the ringside watching the proceedings and noting in his mind those animals that were genuine and those that were not. Meanwhile Dick, the dealer, ascertained what animal or animals Mr Strong had brought to market, and went along to have a look at the bullock, and so get an idea what sort of animals he would be likely to see if he went over to Mr Strong's farm. Mr Strong, meanwhile, was still at the cow-and-calf ring and knew nothing of this. Later Dick tackled him and tried to do a private deal over the bullock, but as they could not come to terms it was sold by auction and Mr Strong caught the 4.30pm bus from Taunton to Minehead.

Road to Ley Farm

Eighteen

FARMING

T HE largest farm in the district is West Luccombe, farmed by Mr
Richard Clarke. The total acreage is 275, and it includes the hill
farm of Pool. Mr Fred Partridge farms 120 acres at Luccombe itself,
and is in the closest farming contact with the community; farmhouse and
buildings being right in the village itself. Other neighbouring farms
include the hill farms of Ley and Wilmersham, and, in contrast, the small
farm of the late Mr Strong at Luccombe Mill.

Before the war Mr Partridge had forty to forty-five acres under plough,
but now he has as many as seventy-five acres. He favours growing a
number of different crops, so that if one fails there is always another to
fall back on. The medium light soil is very well suited to the cultivation
of barley, and this is his chief crop; he also grows oats, roots, beans,
wheat, and rape. The barley is grown for sale, but he grows only sufficient of the other crops to satisfy the needs of his own stock.

He runs about forty-two bullocks, and rears ten to twelve calves each
year, selling a corresponding number of store cattle. Before the war, when
cattle cake was available and less pasture was under plough, he kept on
his store beasts and fatted them off himself; but in wartime this was
impossible owing to shortage of feeding-stuffs. Many of the store beasts
are bought and turned out on Minehead marshes, where they will fat and
be ready to kill in four to five weeks. There are a hundred and ten
breeding ewes on this farm, of the Exmoor Horn breed, and a Blackface
ram is kept as this cross produces a heavier animal suitable for fattening.
The ewes are kept until they are five years old and then sold as draught
sheep. Each year the farmer picks out his draught sheep and any old
'lacers' and keeps back an equal number of ewe lambs from the flock;
each year the flock is turned out on Dunkery for the summer months,
and there they remain until the cold weather sets in and they begin to
make their way to the farm. A certain gate is kept open, and the flock
comes back of its own accord, the farmer only finding it necessary to
round up a few stragglers at the end. The draught sheep are mostly taken
up to Salisbury Plain, where the milder climate soon fattens them off; or
they may be kept on by the buyers to lamb for one more season before
being fattened. The bullocks are also turned out to hill during the
summer, and for this purpose Mr Partridge takes ground at Simonsbath.

Before the war he kept about two thousand poultry and reckoned to
pick up five hundred eggs a day, but the number had to be drastically
reduced owing to lack of staff and feeding-stuffs. There are no pigs on
this farm. Mr Partridge says that pigs and poultry do not agree.

He has been running the farm with the help of a carter and a land-girl.
He has two working horses, but generally uses only one of them, for he
is well equipped with all modern machinery and does not need to
borrow from his neighbours or the War Agricultural Committee. A pony
is kept for shepherding.

Mr Partridge has won a number of prizes at agricultural shows. In
1931, he took first prize at Minehead Fat Stock Show, in the class for two-
year-old bullocks, and first prize in the three-year-old class. In 1938, he
won a silver cup as second prize for a dog hound walked by him for the

Devon and Somerset Staghounds. In 1934, he had a first prize for a dog hound with the Minehead Harriers. He is a very keen sporting farmer and has a collection of over twenty silver teaspoons presented by the different hunts for the puppies he has walked.

When hounds were meeting anywhere near Luccombe he used to take his puppy, Artful, and let it hunt with the pack. On one occasion his hound got a hind away on its own. He and two or three others followed the hound, and after an exciting hunt came up with and killed their quarry. This feat was recorded in the local and London papers. Now the war is over he hopes to keep a hunter or two again, walk puppies once more, and have a day off now and again for hunting.

Mr Richard Clarke farms West Luccombe, with a total acreage of 275. It is a mixed farm, mainly arable. Seventy acres of land at Pool are used entirely for summer grazing, more than half this farm having been re-seeded directly before and during the war.

There is a good deal of arable land at West Luccombe, and the chief cereal crop is malting barley, for which Mr Clarke has taken the Bristol championship. Wheat, oats, beans, roots and very small quantities of sugarbeet and potatoes are also grown. Mr Clarke put in one acre of sugar-beet, which yielded seventeen tons of washed beet; this is an exceptionally good yield, twelve tons being considered good. The crop pays well but is very awkward to harvest, as it comes at a time when all available labour on the farm is needed for other things. The farmer contracts with the factory to grow the beet and delivers to the factory; the pulp is useful for animal feeding-stuff, and, at a pre-arranged charge, the farmer may buy back pulp from the factory in proportion to the amount of beet he has sold them.

The usual rotation of crops is a four-year plan, but Mr Clarke has tried out a five-year plan and finds that it works out well. Starting with roots the first year, corn the second year, corn again the third year, undersown with grass-seed, including clover; this is mown in the fourth year and makes the hard seeds hay; the fifth year it is put down to 'ley' corn. Oats and barley are sown in the spring and wheat in the autumn, barley is usually the first crop to be planted and the last to be harvested, but practice varies with the season. Out of a hundred and eight acres at present down to corn Mr Clarke estimates that twenty acres will provide the necessary food for his own stock. The rest will be sold, and it is the corn cheque which is relied on to pay the wages.

This farm carries eighty head of Devon and cross-bred cattle. They breed all their own stock and buy in extra calves to rear at about two weeks old. These are sold as store beasts at two years old. About twenty-three to thirty-five are sold yearly, and the same number of calves reared. Cows are kept only for rearing calves and supplying enough milk for the farmer and his employees.

Sheep and lambs number about four hundred. There are a hundred and sixty ewes, Dorset Down, and Devon Close-wool cross. About a hundred and fifty lambs are fatted off each year by folding them on the roots, the best of the ewe lambs being retained in the flock. Cattle and sheep are sent up on the hill from May until August, so that every available acre can be laid up for mowing. During the winter months the bullocks are kept in the yards on a plentiful supply of straw, which becomes well trodden and makes first-class manure to go back on the land. The farm is worked with five men and a land-girl. Mr Clarke's father farmed the land before him, so the present Mr Clarke has lived on the farm all his life and has an intimate knowledge of his land. He is well equipped with modern farming machinery and keeps the only registered pedigree bull in the district – a Devon; the only other bull available is a Pole Angus at Holt Ball Farm, but the majority of farmers prefer to use the Devon.

Of all the farmers in Luccombe district, Mr Clarke appears to be the most up to date in his methods. West Luccombe is a roadside farm on the way from Horner to the main Porlock–Minehead road and is one mile from Porlock. The outbuildings are in good repair, close to the house and with direct access to the road.

Mr Clarke's knowledge of the land is of great value to him, and he puts it to good use. Since his marriage eight or ten years ago (to a London girl he is said to have met when she brought a camp of Girl Guides to the district) he has run the farm on his own. Before that he farmed under his father. He was a young man in his early twenties when he took over this big farm, and he has put all his energy into the fruitful cultivation of his land.

Two years ago his health broke down, and though he is now perfectly fit again he has been advised to take a smaller farm and is hoping to take over a farm at Tivington, at present farmed by a relative.

Mr Clarke studies his farm accounts very carefully and knows approximately what degree of profit he can expect to make for each crop harvested and for livestock brought to saleable age. The crop rotation practised on the farm was a four-year plan, but when war came and farmers were asked to produce more crops, he then decided to try out his five-year plan. This change-over entailed much careful thought and extra work, but he is achieving good results and still keeping his land in good heart.

The Porlock Vale is very well suited to the growing of malting barley, but even in this small area some farms – those close to the coast, for the most part – are definitely more suitable than others. West Luccombe has never been considered one of the best barley-growing farms in the area, but Mr Clarke decided he would do his utmost, and recently he was awarded the Bristol Championship. He is very proud of this, for many neighbouring farmers are older relatives who have been farming years longer than he has. Sugar-beet is another crop with which he has been very successful. The War Agricultural Committee asked him to grow the crop, and rather than put it in anywhere, he chose the very best piece of land he had, arguing that as he had to grow the crop he would grow the finest possible and make it profitable, and in this he entirely succeeded.

Ley Farm is 850 feet above sea-level, and lies in a sheltered dip between Ley Hill (1041 feet) and Woodcock's Ley (1039 feet), facing out across Porlock Bay to the Bristol Channel.

This hill farm is owned and run by Miss Ridler, who has lived on the farm all her life, and was previously housekeeper to Mr Floyd, her uncle by marriage, who left her the farm at his death. The thirty acres of arable land on this farm are used to produce winter food for the stock, and no crops are grown to sell. The principal crop here is oats, which are threshed out on the farm with their own threshing-machine; about four acres of barley are grown yearly, which are used for feeding the pigs; one and a quarter acres of wheat is also grown, so as to have straw for thatching. This is threshed by the very old-fashioned method of combing.

It is principally a sheep farm and carries a flock of three hundred. It also carries twenty bullocks, selling an average of eight stores yearly. One pig is reared annually to fat for the house and one breeding sow is kept, so that there is a constant supply of small pigs to sell.

There are four workers on the farm. Three working horses are kept, and it is only occasionally found necessary to call in the help of a tractor. During the summer months the stock is turned out to graze on the hill. Some years ago the farm always ran about fifteen ponies on the hill, but owing to lack of demand this number has now fallen to one. One of the four workers on this farm is Alfie Keal, who has worked here all his life, starting as a schoolboy and doing weekends only. At first he and his wife lived at the farm, but when their eldest child, now fifteen, became old enough for school they moved down to Porlock because the one-and-a-half miles of steep road was too much for a child to do twice daily. Alfie walks to work each morning, has all his meals at the farm, and returns home in the evening to tend his own garden.

Wilmersham Farm, a thousand feet above sea-level, looks across the wooded coombe to the isolated little church and farm of Stoke Pero. It is another sheep-raising farm of a hundred and seventy acres and is farmed by Mr Westcott. There are three hundred sheep, thirty head of bullock, and fifty acres of arable land.

During one year twenty-four acres of heather have been put under the plough. It will be put into roots three years in succession, and sheep will be folded on it to eat it off. This will help to break up the sod and so make it fit for planting a grass mixture containing white clover. New grass, such as Mr Westcott hopes to obtain, will be excellent for fatting lambs, which can be brought in off the hill and fatted off in three to four weeks on good new pasture.

Mr Westcott says that many of his neighbours are laughing at him for taking the trouble to cultivate this rough land, but he has high hopes that before long he will be able to prove to them that his trouble has not been in vain. It is puzzling to know why many farmers are loath to plough up rough land now that the War Agricultural Committee has brought the necessary machinery to them. It is not a new experiment, for it was done half a century ago on the barren waste around Simonsbath by the late Sir Frederick Knight, and during the last few years hundreds of acres the Exford side of Simonsbath have been reclaimed by Sir Robert Cohn, of Honeymead, but both these men are wealthy and can afford to experiment and to lose if necessary.

Up to the end of 1944, Luccombe Mill was farmed by the late Mr Strong. There are twenty acres of arable land, and Mr Strong grew barley, wheat, oats, beans, mangolds, swedes, and turnips, more oats and barley being grown than wheat and roots, because he needed the oat straw particularly for feeding his bullocks. He had only farmed the land for three years, and during that time his health had never been good, so that he had not got his programme as he would have liked. He had generally worked a four-year rotation of crops, but hoped at Luccombe to introduce a catch crop and, where the soil is fertile, to have two years of corn in succession or a two-years' ley of grasses. He had no sheep, but when he had more roots than he needed for his bullocks he took in sheep to eat them off.

He kept thirty head of cattle, reared all his own calves, and sold off his steers as stores, and occasionally sold a heifer and calf, buying in young heifer calves to replace when necessary; of the thirty cattle, nine were milking cows. During the summer months he put out some of his young stock to Codsend moor on the other side of Dunkery Beacon, paying the owner grazing rights; the owner of this grazing also receives a Government subsidy of three pounds per head for each bullock grazed for more than five months of the year. Mr Strong was helped by Mervyn Arscott. He kept two working horses and was well equipped with machinery, but not all of it was usable at Luccombe Mill as the land is too hilly and the fields are small.

When the Strongs were first married they lived at a fairly large farm belonging to Lieutenant-Colonel Dennis Boles, at Bagborough, near Taunton. Mr Strong had lived and farmed in that district all his life, and his wife, a Taunton woman, is said to have known him and his family for many years. However, soon after their marriage they were accepted as tenants for the small hilly farm known as Luccombe Mill, a rather different proposition from the farm at Bagborough where there are large flat fields. Mr Strong took a very great interest in the problems of his new farm; in the soil and in what crops it was capable of producing. He died suddenly at the beginning of 1945.

It is at Cloutsham Farm that the Devon and Somerset Staghounds hold their opening meet of the summer stag-hunting season, during the first or second week in August. This farm was originally two thatched cottages occupied by shepherds, who tended the sheep and ponies running on the surrounding hills. The property belonged to the late Sir Thomas Acland and was a very favourite spot of his. He always reserved furnished rooms here and loved to sit on the wooden verandah, which he had specially built on to the house so that he could watch the deer moving on the steep wooded slopes of East Water coombe opposite. The old farmhouse was large enough to allow the tenant to take in paying guests, and the deer, the solitude, and the beautiful scenery have attracted many artists, among them Lionel Edwards and Cecil Aldin. Lionel Edwards describes an Exmoor farm, which might be Cloutsham, in his recent book, Scarlet and Corduroy. Old Mrs Keal at one time worked at Cloutsham as cook, and well remembers Mr Edwards. As souvenirs of his visits there she has several sporting prints and a very large reprint of a stag's head painted by him and signed. Her son Eddie is the proud possessor of an ordinary white dinner plate on which Lionel Edwards drew the head of a stag, using candle smoke and a match. In 1916 all the original buildings were destroyed by fire, but were subsequently rebuilt as near as possible to the original design – though without the thatched roof – possibly larger, and with the interior brought more up to date. For the past four years Cloutsham has been let to Hector Heywood, harbourer to the Devon and Somerset Staghounds. It stands completely on its own, two-and-a-half miles from Luccombe, on the road to Exford. The house stands directly on the road and is on the edge of the steep wooded coombe of East Water. About sixty acres of land go with the house. Cloutsham is an ideal place from which to carry out the job of harbourer, as it is in the heart of the red deer country. The wooded coombe of the East Water and that of the Horner Water meet at Cloutsham Clamour, about a mile below Cloutsham Farm. These two coombes are well known as the favourite haunt of deer.

Owing to wartime regulations, Mr Heywood was obliged to plough up much of his land. He keeps a few bullocks, but his farm can best be described as a sheep and pony ranch. Since before the last war, and till Hector Heywood took over, the farm had been let to the Forster family. Mr Forster was a keen sportsman and kept sheep and horses while his wife let rooms, charging about six guineas a week. Then Mr Forster was drowned in the hunting accident described earlier, and Mrs Forster carried on alone.

Edward and Albert Staddon, who live with their two cripple sisters in the Square, Luccombe, farm the sixty-odd acres of glebe land, plus another fourteen acres, making a total acreage of seventy-four altogether. There are twenty-eight acres of arable land, nine acres of roots, eight acres of barley, seven acres of oats, and four acres of wheat. They keep fifteen head of cattle, the majority of which are Devons, but there are one or two Devon Shorthorn crosses, and of these cows nine are milking and six are heifers. Mr Staddon goes in for milk production and supplies all the village, his surplus being collected daily by the milk lorry. He is not bothered with a milk-round, as all his customers call for their own milk; generally speaking, the children go for the milk for their own households and assist their neighbours where there are no children. Daphne Prescott, for instance, fetches her grandparents' milk as well as her mother's; she is invariably accompanied by her friend Joan Howard, whose job it is to fetch the milk for the Howard household. Tony Howard gets milk for Miss Sims and Mrs Tame, but is not always to be relied on, and they often find they have to get their own.

Mr Staddon works the farm with two horses. He does not rear any calves unless a cow has a particularly good heifer calf – then he might rear it, but for the most part, he sells his calves when they are about two to four weeks old. Sometimes he will sell an old cow and her calf together and replace them with a freshly calved heifer.

He also keeps about ninety sheep, of which forty are ewes and fifty lambs, and he sells his lambs in the early spring when they are about one year old. During the summer the sheep feed in the meadows, but from November to March they are put on to roots, as he does not take hill grazing.

The year-old fat lambs are sold in the grading-market. Talking about this market while the war was still on and the National Government still in power, Mr Edward Staddon said:

> That's one good thing the Government has done – given us a sure market, so that if you rears a good sheep you knows you'll get a fair price for 'un, because it's all graded and you get what it's worth.
> Before grading came in you could sometimes buy sheep in the autumn and keep them all the winter on your best roots, then when you came to sell them again in the spring only get a matter of three to five shillings more'n you paid for 'un. Like that you were out of pocket. But after the war what's going to happen? That's what I'd like to know. The town people always expects their food to be cheap. They've taken high prices for granted now there's a war on, but food will be the first thing they'll expect to buy cheaper after the war.

This is not really a proper 'farm'. The buildings which the Staddons use are scattered all over the village. The cowsheds are up Stony Street just beyond the church, the linney is in the field behind the rectory, and the barns and stabling are next to Mr Partridge's buildings. The house which the Staddons occupy is a fair-sized one, built about fifty years ago, for a gentleman's country cottage, but not used as such for long. It is semi-detached, and Miss Sims lives next door in the smaller house.

Ford on the road from Webber's Post to Cloutsham

The lane to Selworthy

Pipe carrying Luccombe's water supply from a spring in the woods.

Nineteen
THE VILLAGE SCHOOL

THE village school is a Church school, so those who have grown up in Luccombe have been brought up in the traditions of the Church of England rather than of any other denomination. It was built about half a century ago, and consists of a square building made from large blocks of the local hard red ironstone. There is one large school-room, approximately twenty-four feet by twenty feet, and a small entrance porch, containing a porcelain sink and a cold-water tap, where the children hang their coats.

The schoolroom is heated by a slow-combustion coke stove and has large windows at both ends of the room. The walls are panelled halfway up, and above that are decorated with instructional pictures and examples of the children's own drawings. A weather chart on the wall is filled in every day with wind direction, temperature, cloudy or fine, sun or no sun, state of roads, dew or mist, and the exact time of the recording.

For the past fifteen years the school has been run by Miss Sims, a native of Staffordshire. Miss Sims came to Luccombe at the age of thirty-one, having previously taught in Minehead. She is fond of children and takes a pride and interest in her job. In return the children respect and like her; they share their confidence with her, and she has helped them out of many scrapes. She gets on perhaps less well with the parents, because she is outspoken and dislikes interference. She still retains her North-country accent and does not mix with the village people, who know little or nothing about her affairs.

She had, during the war, twenty pupils of ages ranging from five to fourteen. This was rather above the usual peacetime number, since seven were evacuees. All the children but two came from the village itself and had only a very short walk to school. The only two children having a long walk lived at Holt, one and a quarter miles from Luccombe on the way to Tivington.

One teacher is meant to manage this very mixed age group alone, but owing to indifferent health, Miss Sims is allowed the help of a paid moni-tress. Nora Arscott, a Luccombe girl, aged about twenty, fills this post. She is an ex-pupil of the school and finished her own education there six years ago and has been helping Miss Sims ever since.

When Miss Sims took over the school it was in a very bad state of repair. There was a hole under the door, due to a well-worn step, which would let in a dog. She found out that it had not been repaired for nineteen years and suggested to the governors that certain repairs should be undertaken. They apparently replied in horror that no other teacher had ever complained and surely what was good enough for them should be good enough for her. She accordingly wrote to the County Council, and the work was soon put in hand. That was fifteen years ago, and nothing has been done since. As one ten-year-old pupil succinctly put it in a recent essay, "In the school are lots of pictures. The school wants a paint though."

However, redecoration is about to be put in hand.

The curriculum includes spelling, reading, writing, composition, geography, history, scripture, nature study, sums, physical exercises, and gardening; woodwork takes place once a week at Porlock. There is a garden attached to the school and each pupil has a patch for which he is personally responsible. The tricky business of manipulating so wide a range of ages is partly solved by these gardens, and Miss Sims gives the young ones their first lessons in reading while the older ones are working outside.

Reading books are based on instructional subjects, on tales of exploration and history, and a series of questions is asked at the end of each lesson. Judging from a set of the children's essays the standard of composition, writing, spelling, and punctuation is shown to be high and would bear comparison with many much better equipped schools. Arithmetic is the subject over which there is greatest difficulty. This Miss Sims accounts for by the fact that the children never have occasion to handle money; they have no bus fares to pay, they never go to the pictures alone, and if they are sent to the village shop for anything it is usually paid for later by their parents. They do not receive regular pocket-money, because there is little here to spend it on. The girls are taught to darn and mend, and both boys and girls learn knitting.

Luccombe children have never excelled at scholarship examinations, and Miss Sims is strongly against them. It appears that examiners are often influenced by the details of the parents' circumstances, for which they ask, and that the child of a farmhand stands a poor chance. Miss Sims's own idea in educating the children is to concentrate on reading and spelling, for she believes any child who can read well has the opportunity of continuing his own education after leaving school.

When Nora Arscott was given the job of helping Miss Sims in the school there was some criticism among the villagers. They said they paid rates (rents here are from 2s.6d. to 3s.6d. per week inclusive!) and expected a qualified teacher to be provided. Some of the villagers are quite severely critical of the school:

> I think the education is shocking. The Government ought to give us a proper school or else arrange for the children to go to Minehead. It stands to reason that they can't learn properly with only one teacher and one classroom. My big boy is thirteen and he knows nothing. It's too far for them to walk one-and-a-half miles to catch the Minehead bus in the winter. A bus should be brought here, and the village school should be turned into an infants' school. (Housekeeper to forestry worker.)
>
> They learns nothing no good at school. (Farm labourer's wife.)
>
> Well, if they learns nothing, at least we know where we are. (Estate workman's wife.)

On the other hand, the mother of a boy who has passed on to Minehead County School after attending the village school until he was eleven, says:

> Well, I don't think they do too badly. My boy gets on all right at the secondary school in Minehead. He was backward with his sums at first as he hadn't done decimals and fractions.

The animus against the school is partly due, no doubt, to the fact that Miss Sims is a 'stranger'. The school, the church, and the shop are the only institutions in the village, and both church and school tend to attract criticism. Miss Sims herself feels that the parents take very little interest in their children's schooling:

It's hopeless trying to keep them disciplined. They don't get any discipline at home – the parents just want them out of the way. You should see them in the summer, when the visitors are here. They just run wild. You can't do anything with them.

At the age of eleven the children have the option of passing on to the secondary schools at Minehead, either the free Council School, or the County School, where fees are payable. At present there are three children attending Minehead schools from Luccombe. In the winter they cycle or walk to Brackley Steps (one-and-a-quarter miles) and catch the 8.41am bus from there. In fine weather they cycle all the way.

If you ask a Luccombe child what he wants to do when he leaves school he will probably say he wants to go on the land and do the same job as his father. A girl will very likely want to go into service. Miss Sims thinks this desire to follow in their mother's or father's footsteps is due to lack of ambition:

They don't have to go to Minehead. Some of them don't want to go. I usually say to the boys when they get old enough – "Well, do you want to go to Minehead or do you want to stay in my cissie school?" But most of them don't care. As long as they can leave school and go on the farm, that's all that worries them. And the parents don't bother. It's funny how they all want to be farmers. There's hardly one with a spark of ambition to raise themselves from the level of their parents. The inspector asked them what they'd like to be, and they all said, "On the farm, like Dad." They just want to be the same as their father, and the same as *his* father. No initiative to go further. I like what one boy said, though, when asked what he wanted to be. "A boss", he said. Or, at least, he didn't use that word. "A maister" is the word they use round here.

In these comments of Miss Sims on the children's lack of ambition appears the persistent bad influence of the nineteenth-century mania for urbanizing country people. It does not seem to occur to anyone that a farmer requires a different sort of education from a clerk and that it is the standardization of education that should be deplored. For there is a real and deep contentment with life in Luccombe. Peter Howard, aged ten, wrote in a free composition on Luccombe:

I live in the little village of Luccombe. It is a beautiful place. I have lived here ever since I was born. My house is a Council cottage. Luccombe lies at the foot of Dunkery Beacon. It is spring now, and the village is a beautiful sight. In the village is a small shop where tin goods and sweets are sold.

Opposite the shop is a church, it is a very old one. Monks built it years ago, they lived at Cleeve Abbey. There is a school in the village too. Luccombe is five miles from Minehead and three from Porlock. There are twenty-nine houses. My house is not very old. The blossom is on the apple-trees, and it looks pretty. There are two farms.

And this was written by an evacuee boy of thirteen:

I live in a cottage not far from Luccombe. I have been here for five years. The village itself is very pretty, but some of the people in Luccombe are fond of getting other people and the children into trouble. When anyone goes up the road they all stare as if they haven't seen you before... There is a little shop, and it has not got half what you want. There are not many houses in Luccombe because there are not very many people. The people have to go out to work to get a living.

In common with the adults, the boys of the village have a lively feeling for the countryside and the land. They lead an open-air life, pick flowers and whortleberries in season, play by the streams and in the woods, and often, while they are still at school, help on the farms. Like the adults they have an eye for the beauty of their everyday environment, and little reason to want to change. The majority of villagers do not, in fact, care very much about the education of their children. As long as they are good labourers, that is the main thing. The children themselves are not, on the whole, ambitious for a town life. They enjoy most lessons in the open air and helping with gardens.

"I hate school," said one of the boys, "although we had a nice day today. I hate arithmetic."

"What do you like?"

"I like to do my garden. I'm going to be a farmer, you see."

And one of the girls:

"What are you going to do when you leave school?"

"Go into service. I hope so, anyway."

Like all children, they relate their lessons to their surroundings. Miss Sims was giving a Scripture lesson on the Temptation and telling the children that Jesus went away by Himself into the wilderness. They didn't know what a wilderness was, so she said, "You know what it's like on Dunkery, don't you – wild waste land with no trees or fields? Well, the wilderness was like that.

Next day she asked them questions on the previous day's lesson:

"Where did Jesus go after the Temptation?" Freddie Wylde: "Up on Dunkery, Miss."

One or two of the parents have other ideas for their children, notably the Howards and the Arscotts. Mrs Howard has sent Basil to the County School, and she has hopes that Joan (age eight) will be a schoolmistress:

Joan herself wants to be a nurse. I don't know whether it's the war or not. She's still a baby. I'd like to see her be a schoolmistress myself. She's a domineering little thing, and that's what you want. She'll show them she's boss. I'd like her to be a schoolmistress.

But this is the exception. Most of the village grumbling about the school is based more on the fact that it is the only local institution to grumble at than on any real anxiety for the children's education. And perhaps the older ones envy the freedom the children get, compared with their own young days. They have outdoor lessons in the fine weather, and Miss Sims encourages them to confide in her and treat her in an informal way. But some villagers lacking in understanding will comment on a sunny afternoon when pupils and teacher are outside leaning on the rails at the edge of the road, "Oh, they never do nothing in there." That is the stereotyped grumble, but Mrs Keal, when asked what she thought of the education, was nearer the mark: "Farm lads," she said, "only need to learn three things – read, write, and reckon. They learn everything else by hard work and experience. You can't learn how to farm and look after animals out of a book."

For the rest, the children of Luccombe play very much like any other children anywhere. There appear to be no special local games or traditional jingles, unless snail racing can be counted as a Luccombe pastime.

Twenty
A Glimpse at Luccombe's History

WE have already walked up and down Luccombe's main street of twenty-four houses and visited some of the cottages and their residents, seen some interiors, and learned the various occupations of the villagers; but in order to compare the life of present-day Luccombe with that of former times, and to get some sense of its age and the long continuity of its life, we had best enter the parish church, whose square tower marks its site conspicuously in the plain below the moors and Dunkery Beacon.

Topographically, St Mary's church is the centre of the village. Spiritually, it seems now of little importance to the life of the community. Congregations have dwindled all over the country during the war years, and no doubt the factors which have affected churchgoing elsewhere have played their part in Luccombe too. There are at present eight or nine fairly regular churchgoers: the rector's wife and daughter, three old ladies, two young girls, and a couple of children. A typical congregation on five Sunday mornings in April 1944 numbered twelve adults and six children in the choir. Of this congregation, five of the adults were visitors, three were singing in the choir, leaving four villagers in the body of the church. The rector does not consider a congregation of this size unusually small for present times in proportion to the number of parishioners. Excluding three women and six children in the choir, there were twenty in the church on Easter Sunday morning, three of them visitors. The rector estimates the average Sunday morning congregation at six, with three or four in the afternoons. There are many ancillary reasons why churchgoing should have fallen off. Until the end of 1944 the men had to attend Home Guard parades on Sundays, and, owing to labour shortage, farmers and their wives often have to work that day.

Luccombe church of St Mary stands at the entrance to Stony Street. The tower is very fine, and, according to a report made to the restoration committee in 1894, the tower and the walls of the nave and chancel are the only parts of the present building which remain of the earlier church. Some little time after 1500 the south aisle and chapel were added, and the nave and chancel brought into harmony, with windows and ceilings to correspond. A great deal of Early English work, however, such as the thirteenth-century windows, remains. In the church, as in most of our English parish churches nowadays, hangs a list of the rectors of the church from the earliest times. So much history is suggested to the imaginative reader by a mere perusal of this list that I take the opportunity of giving it here as compiled by Chadwyck Healey from Diocesan registers and other documentary authorities:

> Tempus Edward I. William, persona de Locombe, amerced for the flight from justice of his servant.
>> Edward I. Robert de Luccombe, persona ecclesie de Loccumloe.
>> Edward I. William Roges, on the presentation of Hugh de Luccombe.

1311–12	John de Wamberge, on the presentation of Joan de Luccombe.
1312	John Roges, on the presentation of John de Luccombe.
1316	William de Luccombe, on the presentation of John de Luccombe.
1324	Peter de Horseleigh, on the exchange by William de Luccombe for the Church of Overstowey.
1336	Richard de Morcestre, on the presentation of Oliver St John.
1350	Richard Trewe, presented by Oliver St John, knight.
1412–13	Thomas Twyford, on the exchange by Thomas Polton for the Church of Clyst St George in the diocese of Exeter.
1459	John Croft, upon the death of Thomas Twyford; presented by William St John.
1461	Richard Heycroft, upon the death of John Croft; presented by William St John.
1464	John Peter, on the exchange by Richard Heycroft for the Church of Puckington.
1471	John Combe, upon the death of John Peter; presented by William St John.
1493–94	John Trerice, upon the death of John Combe; presented by John Arundell, of Trerice.
1563	John Bridgwater, M.A., upon the death of the last incumbent; presented by the Queen.
1574	William Maskall, upon the resignation of John Bridgwater; presented by the Queen.
1574–75	Laurence Byam, upon the resignation of William Maskall; presented by the Queen.
1615–16	Henry Byam, S.T.B.
1648	Robert Crosse, Public Preacher.
1654	John Wood, Public Preacher.
1669	John Wood, S.T.B., upon the death of Henry Byam; presented by Thomas Henly, William Scott, and Alexander Blackford.
1687	Thomas Stawell, M.A., on the presentation of John Arundell, esq.
1732	Thomas Hargrave, M.A., presented by William Draycott.
1757	William Willis, LL.B., upon the death of Thomas Hargrave; presented by Richard Lyster, of Rowton, Salop.
1781	Richard Purdy, B.A., upon the death of William Willis; presented by Susannah Wentworth, widow, and Frederick Thomas Wentworth.
1782	Robert (Freke) Gould, on the cession of Richard Purdy; presented by Susannah Wentworth, widow, and Frederick Thomas Wentworth.
1839	Thomas Fisher, M.A., on the death of Robert (Freke) Gould; presented by Sir Thomas Dyke Acland, Bart.
1856	Edward Cox, M.A., on the death of Thomas Fisher; presented by Sir Thomas Dyke Acland, Bart.
1869	James Vivian Bull, M.A., on the death of Edward Cox; presented by Sir Thomas Dyke Acland, Bart.
1891	Henry Dyke Acland, M.A., on the death of J.V. Bull; presented by Sir T.D. Acland, Bart.

I draw attention to the entry, "Robert Crosse, Public Preacher"; 1648 is the date of the first Parliament introducing the Presbyterian system and the sweeping away of prelates. During the Civil War an attempt was made to arrest the rector, Henry Byam. Dragoons were garrisoned on the village by Parliament and a contemporary record says, "At least forty will not only have our hay, but oats, too, for their horses, so that we shall hardly eat hay with our horse ere winter is passed." Byam's wife and daughter were drowned escaping to Wales, but he joined King Charles I at Oxford where, by the latter's orders, he received the degree of D.D. on January 3l, 1642, and accompanied the Prince of Wales, later Charles II, to Jersey, where he remained until the garrison surrendered to Parliament in 1651; as it was, he forfeited his estates as a delinquent. At the Restoration he was reinstated at Luccombe and made Canon of Exeter and Prebendary of Wales.

Another historical event to which church registers bear witness is the Black Death. This plague landed at Melcombe Regis, in Dorset, in August 1338. It reached Somerset in the early Autumn and was at its height in January and February 1349, and its ravages are shown by the excessive mortality of the clergy and the constant succession of fresh institutions of them in the various parishes.

Luccombe during the Civil War was royalist, and five shillings were spent in ale at two "severall times of ringing at the returne of the King". There was a lesser feasting on the proclamation of King James II in 1685. The village was also concerned in the Duke of Monmouth's Rebellion. Three rebels are said to have been hanged at Dunster and two at Porlock, and there are items in the parish accounts for expenses for ringing at King Williams coming to crowning. This brings us to the eighteenth century and the Hanoverian succession. In 1791 the Luccombe church-wardens paid one and sixpence for a prayer for the victory over the Spanish Fleet, and in 1797 five shillings for the victory over the Dutch Fleet, and in 1802 a Mr William Paramore was paid £1.10s.0d. "for a hogshead of sider on the settling of a peace".

Money was spent by the parish on killing hedgehogs, polecats, and foxes, and on poor and medical relief. Some idea of property values is shown by the entry of an expenditure in 1721 of ten pounds in the purchase of a dwelling-house and garden, or backside. The following list of the inhabited houses and the population of the parish of Luccombe shows how fairly constant the population was for the century from 1801; and the rate of rise or decline shown in this list is similar for the whole district, including Oare, Stoke Pero, Culbone, Selworthy, and Porlock; but some time after 1881 Luccombe parted with three houses and a popula-tion of sixteen ceded to Timberscombe and Cutcombe for outlying parts at Harwood and Nackers under the Divided Parishes Act. The size of the Parish of Luccombe at this time is reckoned as 3870 statute acres.

INHABITED HOUSES IN LUCCOMBE

Date	1801	1811	1821	1831	1841
Houses	84	79	86	105	111
Population	457	417	481	546	580
Date	1851	1861	1871	1881	1891
Houses	108	107	107	94	91
Population	512	474	430	348	333

This list, governing the nineteenth century, indicates the astonishing stability of life in this part of the country. Indeed, Luccombe must be con-sidered as one of the villages in England which has changed least from the Norman Conquest in 1066 to the present day. This is partly, of course, due to the fact that it lies in the midst of agricultural country, whose main occupations today remain almost entirely unindustrialized. The majority of the villagers of Luccombe were doing in 1945 very much what their forefathers were doing in 1145. For eight hundred years they have farmed the land, cut wood, and hunted, with a very gradual and slight change of methods. Another reason for this stability is that Luccombe has always been far away and inaccessible both from well-populated Bristol and from London. Nor did it offer much to invaders by sea from Wales or Bristol. It lay in a narrow strip of land between the wide, high, bleak moors and the sea; it had virtually no minerals, no coal, only the produce of forests and fields.

A real demand for more educational facilities made itself felt during the early-nineteenth century. In the middle of the seventeenth century, say about the time of Milton, only two men out of the neighbouring Culbone parish could write their names, and this was typical of them all. In this matter there was very little change from 1618 to 1818, when evidence was given by the clergy about the facilities available in the neighbourhood. Porlock, which then had a population of 633, had only a small day-school supported by voluntary subscriptions consisting of twenty-three children; Oare had fifty-seven without any provision for its six children; at Stoke Pero, with a population of sixty-one, "a few children are taught to read by an old woman who receives parish pay"; at Luccombe, with a population of 417, there was "only a Sunday-school"; in Selworthy, with a population of 458, there were three small schools at which between fifty and sixty children were taught at twopence per week by 'females', also a school for writing and arithmetic seldom containing more than ten or twelve children; the rector adds "the poorer classes are desirous of having more sufficient means of education". In the spring of 1900 there were 150 children in Porlock school; in Luccombe school, 25; in Selworthy school, 84; in Oare, 8; in Culbone, only 4, who should attend at Oare or Porlock, and the children of Stoke Pero go to school at Porlock.

What of the agricultural products during Luccombe's history? The rolls of the bailiff show that in medieval times wheat, great oats, barley, and grey peas were grown; rye was introduced a little later, but there is little mention of orchards until Tudor times, although in 1078 there is mention of a vineyard at Carhampton and another at Minehead, while there was a vineyard at Timberscombe some years earlier. But there is no mention of apples in the bailiffs' rolls of Porlock, "which record minutely everything produced or expended upon the demesnes"; but when we reach the reign of Queen Elizabeth (1558–1603) orchards are constantly referred to.

Apart from agriculture, weaving was for centuries the chief occupation of the people of West Somerset. Almost every village had its fulling or 'tucking' mill, and there was such a mill at Dunster as early as 1078. The other chief industries were tanning and herring fishing in the Bristol Channel; in the eighteenth century were also pottery and tile-kilns in Bossington, and even an iron mill at Horner, and iron-ore was dug from the hill above Luccombe for export to Wales, and the old workings can still be seen overgrown now with bracken and brambles. Red oxen at three years old were used chiefly for agricultural work; at five or six years old they were sold to graziers, the price about 150 years ago being ten to twenty-two pounds each. Men then earned a shilling a day with beer; women, for weeding, etc., sixpence or eightpence. Bad and dear coal came from Wales, as wood during the centuries got steadily scarcer and dearer. In 1794 the best beef, mutton, veal, and lamb could be bought at Taunton at 4d. the lb. in the winter, and 3½d. in the summer. Turkeys were sold at 3s.6d. each, geese at 3s. each, ducks at 2s.6d. the pair, and fowls at 2s. each.

In spite of the freedom from wars which West Somerset shared with the rest of England there was a great deal of local brawling and fighting, frequently ending in violent deaths. Its people in the Middle Ages were headstrong and quarrelsome, and carried arms; there were constant disputes over land, and the King's Sheriffs were often assaulted in the course of carrying out their duties. But with the eighteenth century the tone grew more pacific, the peoples' habits more orderly, the amenities of all greater, and manners became softer and more agreeable.

Twenty One

THE SURROUNDING COUNTRY AND ITS LIFE

IT is only slowly that any place or piece of country reveals itself. Time and acquaintance are necessary, but not the too great familiarity which breeds indifference. The centre of Luccombe is not its so-called Square, which is but the end or beginning (depending on where you start) of a street; it is this street itself, Stony Street, that is Luccombe's highway and only thoroughfare. But it is no thoroughfare in the usual sense of the word, because it ends in a path going up to the moors, to a viewpoint which now belongs to the National Trust and was part of the Acland property known as the Holnicote Estate: beyond this stretches mile upon mile of heather and gorse-covered moorland. Let us start from Luccombe's only shop, on whose front wall still stands the foreign-looking name of Ketnor. (This is an interesting example of the persistence of old things. The name, inexplicable to the villagers themselves and to visitors, undoubtedly comes from the family of Geoffrey de Kitenor, Lord of the neighbouring Culbone, otherwise Kitnor, in AD1242.) Then you have on your left, as you ascend, the small stream, in which we found yellow mullein growing. On your right is the main line of Luccombe's cottages, and it is on the doorsteps of these cottages that you will find two or three of Luccombe's villagers gossiping. When you get up to the slight plateau, called "Webber's Post", where the National Trust has its usual signpost, then if you turn to the north you will see below you, in the hollow between the headland of Minehead on the right and that of Porlock Hill on the left, the large village (or small town) of Porlock, with its church and its attractive shingled tower. A couple of miles beyond Porlock is Porlock Weir and the sea. If it is a clear day you can see from here, across the Bristol Channel, the Welsh cliffs of Glamorgan. Turning from that vista to what lies quite near at your feet, you look down on a ravine, or gully, up the side of which a steep road ascends from the village of Horner, where there are a few houses, several tea gardens, and a fine, now disused, stone mill.

This road will lead to Ley Farm, one of those characteristic hilltop farms where the crops are several weeks later than in the country below. Ley Farm, since her uncle's death, has been farmed by Miss Ridler, and it is on her farm that the tools and implements shown in the photographs are used. If you take the strenuous walk up to Miss Ridler's farm in summer you will arrive with a great thirst. I was taken there by a friend, and Miss Ridler gave us some of her excellent milk in the old kitchen, which was the only part of the house that escaped from a fire several years ago. Nothing could be more attractive than these old kitchens; this one possesses a spit which is still in use. On this farm works Fred Keal, from Luccombe, and it was to see him and extract from him the exact names and uses of the farm tools photographed that we climbed up to Ley Farm. We found no one there except Miss Ridler, who told us we might find them sheep-dipping down in the valley, near Horner. Accordingly we went down to Horner Mill and walked inland alongside the stream, and by good fortune happened on the sheep-dipping at a fenced-off place where the pens and the sheep-dip were placed. A small crowd of village women and children were gathered round, including a policeman. The policeman was a Dorset man who had joined the Somerset constabulary, and he was giving a helping hand to the sheep-dippers. He talked to us and told us a story about Andrew Lang. We learned afterwards that a policeman must always be present as a witness at the sheep-dipping to see it is carried out satisfactorily.

It was a hot sunny August day during that magnificent spell of summer weather in the middle of August 1944, and the scene under the arcade of trees by the murmuring stream was enchanting. Three men conducted the dipping; two seized the sheep, generally by the leg, and threw them in, two or three at a time. The third man, armed with a sort of rake, stood at the side and pushed their heads under the dirty putty-coloured liquid to make sure they were completely immersed, and that the antiseptic got thoroughly into their wool and their heads. They were kept a few minutes in the dip and then were let out through a trapdoor to climb into another pen.

The whole scene might have come straight from Hardy's Woodlanders, for the general character of the setting and the people were the same as in his day, in spite of the local differences between Dorset and Somerset. I do not know whether sheep-dipping was compulsory in Hardy's boyhood, but if not this only shows how completely scientific innovations can be assimilated into the old-established life of the countryside. "New tools for old" does not necessarily mean any radical change in the life and habits of an agricultural region.

For instance, the motor bus is only some thirty years old, and although it has enormously increased the mobility of every hamlet, village, and town throughout Great Britain, and removed the most remote areas from isolation, yet the people of Luccombe remain as definitely rural as ever, in spite of the fact that they now can and do make trips almost once a week to Minehead or Porlock.

Minehead is only about two and a half miles from the corner of the main road where Luccombe villagers pick up the bus. It has a large cinema, many shops, several hotels, and a great number of guest-houses to which holiday-makers from the west, London, Bristol, and even from Wales, come in large numbers every summer, yet it has not been quite spoiled – as, for example, Torquay has in spite of its later sophistication. A row of attractive old houses – not later than 1840 – along the front, together with quite decent later-nineteenth-century terraces in the main street, preserve its old character, and the hideous, ill-proportioned glass fronts of multiple shops are not so much in evidence here as in most of our seaside resorts. I was told that the landlords, the Luttrells (of the famous Psalter), and of Luttrell Castle, at Dunster, take some pains to preserve the amenities of Minehead; but it is questionable whether they are always successful, for I understand that they were responsible for the gasometer being placed at the end of the front near the lifeboat house at the corner of the cliff – which is hardly the ideal place for it. It completely spoils the nicest point along the front, and is west of the town while the prevailing winds are westerly.

I was struck, going into Minehead, by the number of expensive villas along the hillside, all with large gardens facing south and brilliant with a profusion of hydrangeas. All along this coast, and in the plain and small valleys between Luccombe and the sea – particularly at such places as Lynch, and Bossington – there are many good and some beautiful houses with delightful gardens. There is also a chapel of rest at Lynch, once connected with the Abbey of Athelney, but now linked with the parish church of Selworthy. Selworthy church which stands on the steep south slope of Selworthy Beacon, an eminence on the great Minehead Bluff, is the most conspicuous landmark in the whole district. It stands out clearly to the view from many points in the valley. The church (All Saints') has an unusually light interior with large windows and is of admirable proportions. Its barrel-shaped, wooden roof is a fine example of a style prevailing in this part of the country. There is an old hour-glass on the pulpit and some fragments of fine glass – removed, it is said, from Luccombe church some time in the nineteenth century – containing an armoured shield of Sir Nicholas Arundell (in the reign of Edward IV), who died in 1463. The Arundells of Trerice were one of the wealthiest Cornish families and acquired the Manor of East Luccombe by the marriage of Nicholas Arundell with Joan St John. They came into possession of East Luccombe Manor about the time of the Wars of the Roses and retained it throughout nearly three centuries. It then passed, via the Wentworth family, to Sir Thomas D. Acland in 1802, and is now the property of the National Trust by the gift of Sir Richard Acland. At the present moment the rector of Selworthy seems to be rather a lively person, and many of the parishioners of Luccombe like to attend his church in spite of the fact that it is a very steep climb from the valley.

As well as Minehead, the Luccombe villagers have Porlock and Porlock Weir conveniently accessible. Porlock is still a charming town, mainly Tudor in character, with relatively few bad modern buildings. The parish contains about four thousand acres, excluding Bossington's four hundred odd acres and the hundred and ninety-six acres of foreshore and tidal water. It has one main, long, and winding street, where, at the Ship Inn, the new road over the moor through the Lorna Doone country to Lynton branches off to the left, while on the right the road leads on to Porlock Weir. The church, the greater part of which is of the thirteenth century, is on this main road in the centre of the town. Actually the parish of Luccombe inserts a wedge as far as the sea into the parish of Porlock; the origin of this is thought to be the necessity of having access to the sea in the days when the Severn estuary had great importance as a means of communication with all the country east of Luccombe, when road communication from West Somerset eastwards was slow and arduous. How extremely shut off and remote this western country was from the more populous parts of England lying east, and separated by great tracts of difficult country, may be judged from the very name of Luccombe (once spelt Luckham), which means "closed vale".

Even today it is difficult of access and is well shut in by the moor to the south behind it as well as to the west. There are only two gaps to the east; the Minehead road and the road through Wootton Courtney.

In early days the boundaries of manor and of parish pretty well coincided; the lord of the manor of Porlock before the Conquest, as recorded in the *Domesday Survey*, was Algar, son of Leofric, Earl of Mercia. It was transferred after the Norman Conquest to Baldwin, of Exeter, with Rogo, son of Nigel, as underlord, and it remained in possession of the Rogers family until the reign of Edward III, when it passed to the Haringtons. A monument to a Sir John Harington and his wife, known as the "Lord and Lady" monument, is in Porlock church. This John Harington took in the year 1417 a body of eighty-six archers and twenty lancers on one of Henry V's expeditions to France, and some Porlock men were present at the battle of Agincourt, with members of the Harington family. During the Wars of the Roses, Elizabeth, a widow of the fourth Lord Harington, was in possession of the manor of Porlock, and interesting details exist of preparations for a visit she paid to another manor. I quote from Chadwyck Healey's *History*:

Men were set to work to clean the house, to cut fuel, and to mend the windows. Rushes were collected wherewith to strew the hall and chamber, and straw for the lady's bed was bought at the cost of four pence. Honey, oil, and beer were brought for her from Barnstable.

This must have been some time before 1471, for she died in that year. She lived during the reigns of Henry V and Henry VI, and there are accounts extant of John Godde (who was bailiff to the manor of Porlock) for the years 1419–20, 1422–23, and 1424–26, from which many interesting facts of the local economy of Porlock Manor can be learned. For instance, in the year 1422–23 there were sown sixty-five acres of grain as follows: 11 acres of wheat at 2 bushels the acre, 9 acres of barley at 4 bushels the acre, 6 acres of grey peas at 2 bushels the acre, and 39 acres of great oats at 4 bushels the acre. Wheat at the time was sold at 8½d. and 9d. the bushel, barley at 6½d. and 7d. the bushel, grey peas at a shilling the bushel, and great oats at 3s.4d. the quarter. Thirteen shillings and twopence was paid for an ox.

The bailiff took in those times four days to ride to Exeter and back to buy wine. There must have been a good highway to Dunster, for it is on record that he took a wagon and two men to go there to bring back a pipe of wine. As to wages, we find that eightpence was paid for two nights' work in keeping oxen from the corn. At this time, apart from agriculture, there was a considerable trade in herrings at Porlock.

During the sixteenth century there were many tenants holding leases from the Crown, which then came into possession of the manor, owing to the attainder of the Duke of Suffolk. In 1610 it passed into the Rogers, Winter, and Blaythwayt families, and has remained with the Blaythwayt family. The old manor house was destroyed by fire late in the nineteenth century and is represented now by the modern house at Court Place and has become the residence of the farmer of the old manor demesne. Old Porlock church happily remains and, like Selworthy church, has most attractive carved barrel roofs with fine wooden bosses painted in colour. The original church was rebuilt in the thirteenth century by one of the Rogers family, a monument to whom still exists there, it is the effigy of a knight cross-legged, indicating a crusader, or one who has made a pilgrimage to the East. The church was restored in 1890, and, like most parish churches in England, constitutes the best historical record of local life, an almost living memorial from its first rector, John of Rogo, 1297, down to the present day. It bears the uncommon name of St Dubricius. St Dubricius (the Welsh Dyfrig) is supposed to have come from South Wales about AD500 and to have been Archbishop of Caerleon. He is said to have crowned Arthur, afterwards returning to Porlock. He is also supposed to have established large schools of sacred learning on the Wye, where he had a thousand scholars.

We went to morning service at Porlock on Sunday, August 13, 1944, and I was delighted to find that the lessons were exceedingly well read and the church well attended. Service at an old English parish church with a good rector is one of the most pleasing and moving experiences an Englishman, or anyone of British descent, can have. Here alone we can be at the very heart of our local history in its continuity over a period of six or seven centuries. On the gate of the present rector's beautiful garden I noticed, after the service, a small sign saying that all who wish to enter the garden for solitude and meditation are welcome.

It is a couple of miles walk from the village of Porlock to Porlock Weir, or Ware, an attractive little tidal harbour with stone quays, one good hotel, and a small number of houses. There were a few boats there, and coal is still brought in by sea, but as a fishing port it has quite lost the importance it must once have had. Unless something is done it will soon be obstructed, for the beach stretching from Porlock Weir to Bossington is a mass of shingle that is being ever heaped up higher by the tide. The harbour was built about 1422–27 and once had regular communication with Wales, and a resident customs officer. At one time there must have been ship-building here, for there was a charge of three shillings for every boat and six shillings for every barque built on the manor's waste land. Into the small harbour of Porlock Weir were imported, as is shown by the tolls, cattle, sheep, and poultry from Wales and wine, tobacco, raisins, sugar, oranges, and lemons from other countries. The advent of railways in the early-nineteenth century gradually reduced all this flourishing trade, and the port decayed. It once had a chapel, now built into the house at Chapel Knap. In 1811, according to the Porlock parish register, it had a population of 31 males and 56 females; at this time the population of the town of Porlock itself is given as 134 males and 156 females. It is worth mentioning here that the keeping of parish registers in England began in 1501, but was not strictly enjoined until the reign of Henry VIII. The village of Bossington on the other side of the valley had in 1811 about the same population as Porlock Weir – namely, 47 males and 53 females. The register also shows that in 1821 Porlock's population had risen to 769; and in 1831 to 828, a further increase.

We are reminded of Thomas Hardy's descriptions of the instrumental music played in his childhood in the parish churches of Dorsetshire, not so very far away, by the following entries in the Porlock parish accounts. In 1823 the repairing of the bass 'vile' (viol) cost half a guinea, and charges were often made for string. In 1832 there is record of "violencello held by Nicholas Foy, flute held by John Foy" – an interesting example of how musical talent or inclination, however modest, runs in families. How ancient some of our charities are is shown by the record in the small parish of Porlock of Henry Rogers, by his will dated May 8, 1672, bequeathing £600, a very large sum of money in those times, for the parish of Porlock "to be laid out and employed by my trustees and executors for maintaining of the poor there, as I have directed for Cannington." This charity was declared a parochial charity by the Local Government Act of 1894, and is still being administered.

The return by road to the village of Luccombe from Porlock Weir is either via Porlock to the village of Horner at the foot of the Horner Water, where the sheep-dipping took place (during the war of 1939–45 the pleasant houses with their tea gardens near Horner Mill were deprived of most of their custom, which consists in summertime of large numbers of visitors from Wales, Bristol, and London), or we need not go as far inland as Horner, but can keep on the main road to Allerford, passing the saw-mill and farms, with West Luccombe and Holnicote on our right, and visit in turn Allerford, Lynch, and Bossington. At Allerford there is a mill and a chapel. The stone mills of this country, mostly derelict, are still magnificent solid buildings, beautiful in their simplicity and right proportions. It is strange how difficult it is nowadays to equal the buildings of the past; no matter what their function was they achieved then the ideals that the best engineers today achieve in bridges, dams, and similar works, a functional simplicity and rightness which most architects seem unable to put into their domestic and commercial building.

It is interesting as we pass the prosperous and comfortable farms in this neighbourhood to refer to several pertinent entries in the *Exeter Domesday* and the *Great or Exchequer Domesday*:

Two nuns have half a hide and half a virgate in Honecota, which two Thegns held together T.R.E., and William the King granted that land to the said nuns in free alms. Two teams can plough it. They have there in demesne one team and five acres of meadow. It is worth five shillings. It was worth ten shillings when they received it.

From the manor called Hunecota held by Roger de Curcella one fertine of land has been detached and is held by Odo son of Gamelin and Roger wrongly renders geld in respect of it.

Ralph de Limesi holds Alresford.... This manor renders by custom twelve sheep yearly to the King's manor of Clarentone. Until now Ralph has withheld this custom.

Ralph de Limesi holds Bosintune. The church of Athelney held it T.R.E., for the support of the monks and gelded for one hide....

Ralph de Limesi holds Seleurde. Edith the Queen held it T.R.E. and gelded for one hide. There is land for five plough teams. In demesne there are two teams, two serfs, seven villeins and five bordiers with three teams. The mill there renders twenty pence and there are five acres of meadow, sixty acres of pasture and forty acres of wood. It was worth twenty shillings; now twenty-five shillings.

The manors of Hunecota, Alresford, Bosintune, and Seleurde are our present-day villages of Holnicote, Allerford, Bossington, and Selworthy. A stream runs through Allerford, and it is a very pleasant place, with attractive old houses – one being built over the bridge. It has been established by Chadwyck Healey, that Allerford, like Selworthy, has always been part of the manor of Luccombe from the time of Ralph de Limesi, then by inheritance through the Arundell family down to the Aclands. Holnicote, from the time of the earliest records, belonged to a family named Steynings until it was sold in the eighteenth century and, passing through various hands, was bought early in the nineteenth century by Sir Thomas D. Acland.

Continuing seaward to the left from Allerford we pass the old chapel of Lynch, in good order and repair, with farm buildings adjacent, and reach Bossington. The arrival of Methodism in this West Country was celebrated by the opening of a chapel in 1837 at Porlock, and at the end of that century another Methodist chapel was erected at Bossington, on land given by Sir Thomas D. Acland. We are here very near the sea, which lies across a flat shingle beach. Smuggling flourished for centuries in these parts, and one of the many hiding chambers for smuggled goods was accidentally found during the hunt of a fox about 1850; the fox suddenly disappeared between Poole's wood and the Bossington lane, when, by digging, a chamber nine or ten-feet square and the height of a man was found. One of the features of Bossington which struck me most was the number and splendour of the walnut trees alongside the road from Allerford. They are simply magnificent. There are walnut trees near Horner, and almost everywhere in this country, and nobody seems to know why there are so many of them. It is said that many were marked for purchase by the Government for the making of musket stocks during the Crimean War, but that the conclusion of that war just saved them.

A trace of our last war, in the shape of barbed wire, and a mass of empty tins, marking an encampment of soldiers, lies on the beach, which is pretty well deserted at present. We turned back from the beach without regret, it was too cold to bathe, and at the corner of the main Porlock–Minehead road we took the road back to Luccombe, behind which rises Dunkery Hill. After exploring Porlock, Minehead, and the relatively flat country stretching to the sea between them we looked southward again, with our backs to the sea.

We were to find the longer we stayed that it is the moors behind Luccombe which keep their interest most. Their colour and the variety of light and shade on them are magnificent, and if we climb up from

Luccombe they stretch for many miles in utter solitude and quite unspoiled. The valleys cutting through the moor are thickly wooded with many streams, and only here and there is a farm. One of these farms, Cloutsham – used as a hunting lodge by the Aclands during the nineteenth century – has a position of extraordinary beauty. Today it is peacefully inhabited by a farmer, and he has pasture and arable fields in the midst of the heather and the bracken, among which may be seen from time to time the red deer which roam this country. It is said that red deer did not breed within Exmoor forest proper until fences and plantations were made and some shelter thereby provided. This country rivals the Lake District and the moors of Northumberland and Yorkshire for romantic beauty, but is warmer and more sylvan. Farther to the west lies the valley of Oare, which is the celebrated Doone valley of R.D. Blackmore's still famous, though once almost forgotten, novel, *Lorna Doone*. Blackmore was a son of a rector of Oare, and the valley and the country around it is wild and romantic enough even today to suit that delightful and wildly romantic story. The last of the Doone family is supposed to have perished about 1800, and it is said that the original author of the Doone family was a fugitive from the battle of Sedgmoor in 1685.

Horner Valley from Webber's Post

The road into Luccombe

Twenty Two
THE RETURN FROM LUCCOMBE

LEAVING Luccombe in late summer, one sees at first nothing of its surroundings but the narrow, leafy lanes, at times almost tunnels, among which it lies concealed. The red soil at the foot of Exmoor, between the high moors and the waters of the Bristol Channel, is extraordinarily rich and fertile. The little village is surrounded by lush meadows, threaded with cool, crystal-clear streams and separated by narrow, deep lanes – muddy and water-logged in the wet weather, rutted and viewless in summer – twisting, full of corners, in endless meandering between the main roads which cut more directly across the valley bottom. We were motoring there in the trafficless years of 1944, and early 1945, yet even then, going at a walking speed, it seemed decidedly risky when you could only see a few yards ahead; and to meet a single car in any one of these lanes was a perilous adventure and might mean backing for a mile or more before it was possible to pass. When traffic is restored to normal, motoring in and about Luccombe will be highly dangerous. We cannot regret this because it will help to preserve the character and freshness and beauty of this countryside. And the great overhanging highlands of Exmoor, which at Horner and Porlock come down so close to the sea, will remain in their formidable grandeur, and their inaccessibility will prevent any too easy assembling of trippers.

Luccombe should long remain a simple agricultural village surrounded by farms, and offering a complete change of scene to those who visit it from other parts, and a wholly satisfying life to the majority of its inhabitants. The red deer will still be the roving possessors of the moors for the greater part of the year, and the sheep will be brought down annually from the hill farms to be dipped in the streams that run through the wooded coombes into the sea. In a world where so much changes so rapidly as almost to obliterate memory, it is good to think that Time has a foothold in Luccombe where the continuity of the life of individual men and of their families imparts a sense of permanence and duration to all things.

We had a last tea sitting in the garden of a little cottage at Horner, opposite the derelict water-mill, where the stream from Cloutsham runs out of the narrow coombe, into the valley proper. There were several parties having tea, and we were given fresh boiled eggs, which to us, at least, were a rare and unexpected treat. It was with a sense of sadness that we left, and drove out of this beautiful countryside. We passed the turning down to Minehead, and a little farther on passed the end of the Exeter road, which a quarter of a mile away runs through the village of Dunster. We had gone there for lunch one day and had explored the church and the village. Many people know Dunster with its famous round wool-market, its wide street and low delightful houses. The old inn, the Luttrell Arms, dominates the street, for the castle is at the end of the village and out of sight, and the church is hidden away too. The church, built of the same warm red stone as the castle, is most beautiful and contains a remarkable carved wooden screen, said to be the longest in England. We saw the church on the eve of a feast day, and it was marvellously decorated with flowers. The sun streamed in through the open door which leads into the old monks' garden. Enclosed with a wall, sheltered and very fertile, this little patch of ground was more packed with flowers than would seem possible – there was every colour and scent. We met and talked to the vicar, who invited us to go up to the vicarage garden, which overlooks the church, to see the view from the lawn. This garden, too, was wonderfully cared for, and from the lawn outside the house we looked down on the village. Like Luccombe – although it is itself on a hill – Dunster is surrounded by other taller hills and is remarkably shut in and protected. In its houses and streets it feels safe and as unassailable as when the power of the castle was a reality.

But to return to our homeward road. We left Minehead and Dunster behind and drove back through Coleridge's village of Nether Stowey, and past Bridgwater, that ancient seaport and haven of seafaring men, on to Street and Glastonbury. Glastonbury, with its romantic associations with the earliest times of our Church history and the Arthurian legends, and Street, that peaceful little town, with its modern paternally run factory equipped with canteens, swimming-pool, sports-ground, all breathing an air of wholesome and almost vegetable profit, make a most striking contrast typifying ancient and modern in the space of a few miles. But Street is a milestone in the journey to Luccombe, for it is about as far as a sensible traveller by road will want to go in one day, whether proceeding west from London to Luccombe, or vice versa. We stayed that night at Street. Next day our road took us through upland country, rich and fertile, studded with prosperous farms, as far as Shaftesbury. Here we hoped to get morning coffee, but in vain. With true English self-sufficiency and lack of geniality to travellers (who ought to be more wedded to their own cities and firesides!) no refreshment was to be had, not even at the main hotel, which displayed its opulent but somewhat tarnished Victorian splendour only indoors, beyond the bars which were not yet open. Long may it rest intact! Leaving Shaftesbury in its isolation, with a deep sigh we refreshed ourselves in plentitude with the only commodity available – lovely, unspoiled farming country, still full of woods, fields, and beautiful old houses.

It was mostly downhill to Salisbury, where we visited the gaunt and impressive cathedral, but Salisbury, for all its splendour, has something of a bleak austerity and lacks, at a superficial acquaintance, the warmth and friendliness of Winchester. Tired with viewing the magnificent cathedral with all its military glories, we travelled on, and suddenly at a hillside came across a glorious, immense field of strawberries. We inquired and obtained four baskets, freshly picked while we waited, of excellent fruit for the price of 2s.6d. each. When we got to London we found the price of a similar basketful was fifteen shillings. Farther on, at the large village of Alresford, we found a tea shop open and got an excellent tea, which restored us. From Alresford to London was a journey without incident, and we arrived just as the oil-gauge of our car showed us that trouble was near.

Thus, within a day, we had travelled from a country which Shakespeare might have recognized as little changed from his own day to the London that had just survived and triumphed over the German Blitz of 1939–45.

Looking over the Holnicote Estate from Selworthy to Dunkery in the 1930s   *Kinglsey Tayler*

PART THREE

THE NATIONAL PARK COMES TO 'EXMOOR VILLAGE'

by Brian Pearce

THE book title of *Exmoor Village* is in some ways appropriate and not in others. Luccombe was chosen not because it was typical of Exmoor or of Britain as a whole but because it was unusual. It was unusual in the way that it had been unspoilt and largely unchanged in its way of life for most of the century. Lacking in industry, far from cities and protected by the National Trust, it was sheltered from change. Even the Second World War had not affected it greatly. It was dependant upon farming, so many workers stayed in the village during the war. The residents seemed happy in their lot, not particularly wanting change or experience of the outside world but the book suggested that discontentment was creeping in. At the end of the war most of the country was looking forward to a 'Better Britain' and it is unlikely that the movement for change would not have affected Luccombe. People were wanting better housing, pensions, education, a National Health service and continued Government support for farming. Class barriers were breaking down, nationalisation was beginning and there was an expectation of more public access to private property. National Parks were part of this movement.

It is strange that Luccombe people seemed to care little of Sir Richard Acland, who had been their landlord since the beginning of the war. Even though an absentee landlord, he was a well-known and respected local MP. Their minds still harked back to the last patriarchal Acland – Charles Thomas Dyke Acland – who liked to be called 'Sir Thomas' but was affectionately known as 'Charlie'. When he took over the estate in 1898 there had been a 'Sir Thomas' in charge for 170 years and he looked upon running the estate as part of a feudal tradition. Holnicote was just part of his properties, which amounted to 36,000 acres throughout the West Country. Yet 'Charlie' was a Liberal MP - along with his younger brother, Arthur, and Arthur's son, Francis.

'Charlie' died childless in 1919 and Arthur inherited the estate. However, their father had made it impossible for Arthur to sell off any property. Under the circumstances 'Charlie' had seen fit to lease the estate to the National Trust in 1917. The unusual 500 year lease enabled Arthur to run the estate and gain an income from it. Arthur had resented his lack of inheritance but his son, Francis, was much more of a modern Liberal and welcomed the estate having public ownership. In a letter to his wife he wrote: "It's really a magnificent stretch of country. Jolly to think it'll all be national!" Sir Richard, Francis's son, was even more radical. He had been Liberal MP for North Devon since 1935 but was converted to socialism and founded his own 'Common Wealth' party during the war years. He advocated common ownership for moral as well as economic reasons and in 1944 gave all of the land in his possession to the National Trust outright. The people of Luccombe saw no outward difference: they continued to pay their rents to an agent and the estate continued to run in a traditional manner. However, the substantial proportion of Exmoor in the ownership of the National Trust was a factor in the decision to create a National Park, of which the Holnicote Estate was to form the core.

The National Trust had been founded back in 1895 and in 1917 the Holnicote Estate became its largest single property. Its founders had realised that the growth of population, spread of industrialisation and lack of planning was spoiling much of the beauty of the countryside. Their purpose was conservation, education and public access and by the time of *Exmoor Village* many organisations with similar aims had been established. The Council for the Preservation of Rural England, set up in 1926, immediately pressed the Prime Minister, Ramsay MacDonald, for an enquiry into the possibility of National Parks in Britain. He agreed and set up a committee under the chairmanship of Dr Christopher Addison, the Minister for Agriculture.

At the enquiry came the first proposal for Exmoor to become a National Park - from Sir Patrick Abercrombie, the pioneer planner. He included Exmoor in a group of five areas that he felt should have first claim to National Park status. The Addison Report, presented to the Government in April 1931, recommended the establishment of National Parks in England and Wales but in the difficult economic climate of the Depression little could be done. Instead, a Town and Country Planning Act became law. It enabled local authorities to protect trees and woodlands, safeguard historic buildings and designate areas inside which development was controlled. However, there was no practical possibility of this happening without the Government providing resources for administering such areas. For the next ten years the Government was able to fob off the National Parks lobby by saying that local government had the necessary powers. The lack of Government action led to voluntary organisations getting together to form the Standing Committee on National Parks in 1935. This later became the Council for National Parks. Sir Patrick Abercrombie was a member and produced a report "The Case for National Parks in Great Britain", which included Exmoor.

During the Second World War there was a coalition Government and a change of attitude. Lord Justice Scott's report on Land Utilisation in Rural Areas argued for more planning controls and supported proposals for National Parks, including Exmoor. Some members of the Standing Committee on National Parks were civil servants and John Dower, one such member, became a confidant of Lord Reith, the Minister for Town and Country Planning, who invited him to produce proposals for National Parks. The Dower Report, published in 1945, included Exmoor as one of ten areas suitable for inclusion as National Parks. Dower's proposed boundary for Exmoor was initially taken from the areas of moor and heath shown on Land Utilisation Survey maps but added more coastline to the west of the present boundary. He gave a definition of a National Park that remains relevant today:

"an extensive area of beautiful and relatively wild country in which, for the nation's benefit and by appropriate national decision and action,

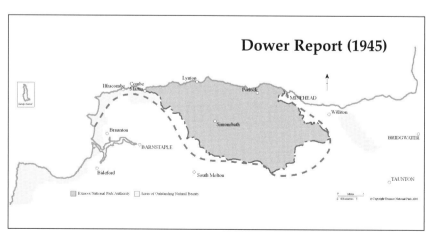

John Dower's suggested boundaries for Exmoor National Park

(a) the characteristic landscape beauty is strictly preserved, (b) access and facilities for public open-air enjoyment are amply provided, (c) wildlife and buildings and places of architectural and historic interest are suitably protected, while (d) established farming use is effectively maintained."

Following the change of government in 1945, Lord Silkin, the new Minister of Town and Country Planning, set up a committee under Sir Arthur Hobhouse to consider how Dower's proposals might be realised. The Hobhouse Report, published in 1947, recommended Exmoor as one of twelve areas most suited to become National Parks. Meanwhile, another Town and Country Planning Act became law. This established development control linked to development plans produced by County Councils. Lord Silkin felt that this legislation gave adequate protection to the countryside and separate National Park legislation was unnecessary. He later changed his mind and gave his name to what became known as the 'Silkin test' on major developments in National Parks. Under the test such developments would only be allowed if they were in the national interest and could not possibly be built elsewhere. Unfortunately the test was never built into legislation and it has been argued that National Park Authorities have been no more successful in fighting large developments than other planning authorities. Through his efforts the National Parks and Access to the Countryside Act was passed in 1949. This set up the National Parks Commission with powers to designate National Parks, Areas of Outstanding Natural Beauty and National Trails. The Commission considered Exmoor as part of the second round of designations suggested by Hobhouse.

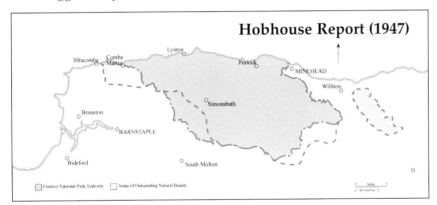

Boundaries of Exmoor National Park suggested by Hobhouse Committee

In September 1952, a month after the Lynmouth flood disaster, a party of four Commissioners came down to Exmoor to walk the Hobhouse boundary, which they modified. The criteria they used were that: the boundary had to follow recognisable features such as roads and had to be based on landscape quality and recreational value. They reported back that in their view Exmoor and the Quantocks were worthy of National Park status and drew up a draft map for consultation with the ten local authorities affected, plus the Ministry of Agriculture and Fisheries, the Commissioners of Crown Lands, the Forestry Commission, the Nature Conservancy, the National Trust and the Standing Committee on National Parks.

The local authorities were mostly opposed to Exmoor becoming a National Park because the Government was not offering them the resources to administer it. Led by Somerset County Council, they argued that a National Park was unnecessary in that there were no major threats to it and no great visitor pressures and Exmoor had remained unspoilt without such status. They were backed by some MPs and Government Ministers, including Harold Macmillan, then Minister of Housing and Local Government, who raised objections in Parliament. The

Commission excluded the Quantocks and areas close to Minehead in the hope that the local authorities would give up their opposition. They intended, when the dust had settled over the issue, to include the Quantocks at a later date. Exmoor was designated as a National Park 27th January 1954 and the Commission sent the Designation Order to Harold Macmillan, for confirmation. Copies were sent to the ten local authorities involved. Most sent in formal objections, forcing the Minister to call for a public enquiry. This was held at Shire Hall, Taunton on 22/23 June. At the enquiry the principal objectors were Devon and Somerset County Councils and Dulverton and Williton Rural District Councils. The County Councils went over their previous objections, namely that:

- as the area was already well protected, it was an unnecessary expense
- it would be easier to administer as an Area of Outstanding Natural Beauty
- if it became a National Park it would be easier to administer if all in Somerset
- the National Park boundaries did not fit local government boundaries, adding to administrative difficulties
- good quality farmland in the Brendon Hills should be excluded
- the proposed National Park did not serve a large population.

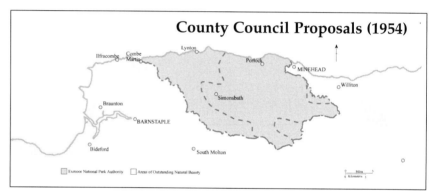

Boundaries of Exmoor National Park suggested by Devon and Somerset County Councils.

The District Councils supported these views, with Dulverton trying to keep out of the National Park, along with the whole of the Brendon Hills. The Ministry of Agriculture and Fisheries wanted the Quantocks and most of the enclosed farmland within the Brendon Hills to be excluded.

In favour of the proposals, the Council for the Preservation of Rural England and the Standing Committee on National Parks wanted a larger area to be within the boundary, including the Quantocks. The Ramblers Association supported this view and the Quantocks 1926 Committee added that the whole of the coastline between the proposed National Park and the Quantocks should be included. Lord Strang, Chairman of the National Parks Commission, felt strongly that if anywhere should become a National Park, it should be Exmoor. It had satisfied all of the selection criteria laid out in the 1949 Act. He also argued that if the 1947 Act had been sufficient to protect the area the 1949 Act would not have been passed. He gave the following reasons why Exmoor should be confirmed as a National Park:

- It was an extensive tract of country, larger than the Pembrokeshire Coast, which was already a National Park and larger than some others suggested by the Hobhouse committee.
- Natural beauty was a matter of taste but Exmoor could offer hills and a very fine coast comparable in beauty to existing National Parks such as the North York Moors.
- Exmoor had few eyesores compared with existing National Parks.

• Exmoor did not have large centres of population on its doorstep but within a 50 mile radius it had more population than Dartmoor, which was already a National Park, and was one of the closest of the proposed National Parks to London.

Confirmation eventually came on 19th October, making Exmoor the country's 8th National Park. The Minister agreed that the boundaries met the criteria set out in the 1949 Act and said that the good agricultural land should be included for scenic reasons. He did not mention the contentious issue of a joint board or anything about the running of the National Park.

Two years after the National Park was confirmed, the new Minister of Housing and Local Government, Duncan Sandys, finally gave notice of the administrative arrangements for Exmoor. The Commission had wanted a joint planning board for Exmoor, as had been created for the Peak District and Lake District. The Government, however, gave in to County Council objections that a board would be adding an unnecessary layer of bureaucracy. In line with all other National Parks that had subsequently been confirmed, Exmoor was given alternative arrangements. It would be administered by separate committees of the two County Councils linked by a Joint Advisory Committee without executive powers. No extra money was available despite the County Councils each having to administer two extra committees. To soften the blow, the Minister did not force them to spend money on extra staff or works. As a result, it was amazing that anything was achieved in the early years to further National Park purposes.

WHAT THE NATIONAL PARK HAS DONE FOR 'EXMOOR VILLAGE'

WHILST there was a great desire amongst British people as a whole for National Parks, the main opposition to them was local. Like many locals, the people of Luccombe would not have been keen on the idea. Because of the concept of National Parks abroad, there was much misunderstanding of how they would operate in Britain. Landowners thought that it was a kind of nationalisation where visitors would roam over their private land, causing damage and leaving gates open. They also feared restrictions on their way of life and work. Some thought that the whole area would become a nature reserve and hunting would be banned. They would also have seen it as unnecessary. A common attitude was that the area had not changed greatly and that it had remained unspoilt without a National Park Authority, so they could manage perfectly well without one. To many, conservation meant preservation and preservation meant leaving things alone – so why was an organisation needed to do nothing? Few would object to designation but many would object to money being spent on an authority.

The Authority has changed much over the years:

From 1954 the work of promoting National Park purposes for Exmoor was undertaken by the National Parks Commission, an independent organisation funded by the Government.

From 1957 Devon and Somerset County Councils formed separate Authorities run by sub-committees of their planning departments with a Joint Advisory Committee. The National Parks Commission provided advice and grant aid.

From 1968 the National Parks Commission was superseded by the Countryside Commission, which continued to provide advice and grant aid whilst the County Councils covered the administration costs.

From 1974 Somerset County Council became the sole National Park Authority, with a separate National Park Department with a committee including representatives from Devon. The Countryside Commission recommended to the relevant government department the level of spending for the National Park and the Exchequer provided 75% of this. The County Councils made up the difference. The Commission continued to provide grants for specific purposes, including up to 80% of the cost of information and education services.

From 1997 the Authority became a freestanding local authority, outside of the County Council system but still with members from County and District Councils, plus representatives of Parish Councils and the nation. The Department for the Environment continued to give a 75% grant to the Authority but gave the District and County Councils the remaining 25% to spend on National Park purposes.

From 1999 the Countryside Commission was superseded by the Countryside Agency.

Following the foot and mouth crisis in 2001, the Department for the Environment became the Department for the Environment, Food and

Rural Affairs. From 2004 it has provided 100% grant direct to the National Park Authority and the process will be reviewed in 2007.

When the first Authorities were set up in 1957, the annual budget was a mere £3,500. The money came out of local rates and expenditure on the National Park had to be weighed against all the other claims on the county budgets – education, police, highways, libraries and other services – and it was never likely to be high in comparison. The system later changed so that most of the money came directly or indirectly from the Exchequer but even today the financial support for the National Park is little more than that for a large school. It soon became apparent, however, that National Park status attracted grants that would help the Councils to undertake works that would in turn attract more income to the area. Within three years the National Park was bringing into the area twice as much as it was costing. The Authority had to submit an annual programme of grant bids to the National Parks Commission for works such as tree planting, removing eyesores and providing car parks, camp sites and accommodation.

The National Park now attracts more funding, both national and European. The main difference between a National Park and any other area of countryside is that it is an area which attracts special grants to fulfil the National Park purposes of conservation, recreation and education. Few locals understood this, although they are recognising it more and more. The Authority has much less power and money than most people imagine and is reliant on local people to conserve the landscape. Most of the early conservation agreements were voluntary agreements which did not involve any form of financial compensation. National Park Committees have always been comprised mostly of local people, including farmers and landowners. The Authority has often been caught in the middle of arguments between conservation, recreation, farming and forestry interests and is more often in the role of arbitrator rather than

Exmoor House in 1963 when it was the offices for Dulverton Rural District Council. It became offices for the National Park Authority in 1974.

ENPA

Keith Bungay, National Park Officer(right) and Lady Gass, Chairman(left) talk to Michael Heseltine to win Government support, late 1980s.

ENPA

taking sides. Arising from the wide consultation for the first National Park Plan, a Consultative Committee of representatives of all major organisations with an interest in the National Park was set up. The National Park Authority has a strategic planning role which enables the threats to Exmoor to be tackled more effectively and with the most efficient use of resources.

Benefits have included:

- Improved maintenance of Rights of Way
- Enhanced protection and higher quality environment
- Rangers on the ground liaising with local people and visitors
- Better interpretation of the area
- Enhanced opportunities for children to understand and enjoy the countryside, particularly for local schools
- Bringing people and organisations together to work towards common goals
- Support to bring special status to the area for funding
- Influencing public organisations or big businesses to respect the character of the area, such as improved design for road schemes or undergrounding of cables
- Support for farmers seeking environmental grants and assistance in delivering environmental improvements on the ground
- Better and integrated public transport and traffic control
- Employment in conservation land management at a time when employment in traditional farming has been falling

The National Park Authority has always had to carry out its function whilst bearing in mind the needs of farming and forestry. Nowadays that works both ways in that other organisations have to bear in mind National Park purposes, whilst the Authority has a broader duty towards the socio-economic well-being of the local community. This means that it should not do anything to the detriment of the latter and it can assist as long as it does not incur any significant expenditure. The Authority takes the view that National Parks are about people in that they are there for their enjoyment. It has to protect the character and special qualities of Exmoor and that these are at largely due to the interaction of people and nature. In order to protect the special qualities it must also protect the way of life of the people who maintain them.

Exmoor Village gives the impression that the way of life in Luccombe had not changed since the beginning of the century, although changes

Exmoor's first three Head Rangers: from left to right, David Beasley, Jim Collins and Bill Gurnett, mid 1990s. Wardens became known as Rangers in the mid 1980s.

ENPA

Hill Gate cottages at Luccombe in the mid 1980s.

Brian Pearce

were afoot, especially in farming. It was largely unspoilt and it was because it was unspoilt that it became a National Park, as this was becoming a rare quality. The village was chosen in order to record a way of life which was fast disappearing. Luccombe has still probably changed less than many other settlements in the country. It is still an estate village, still essentially an agricultural settlement and still unspoilt. A National Park, however, is not a museum and conservation is not the same as preservation. Change cannot be prevented and that is not its purpose. What are protected are the qualities for which the area was designated – its relative wildness, openness, tranquillity, beauty and accessibility. A place can change and still remain beautiful. It takes a lot of hard work to keep it that way and management is the essence of the National Park Authority's work.

In 1940s Luccombe life was much as it was in the mid 19th century but society was changing. Already little of village life was based around the church. The rector and lord of the manor were not as important as before. Motor transport was beginning to dissolve local ties and uproot families. However, there were still few outsiders in the community. Most newcomers came from relatively local places and most people leaving

Luccombe did not go far. Council houses were a new and welcome idea as they kept locals in the village. There was a lack of ambition to go anywhere else but all liked living there and all liked country life. Most married local partners. Boys wanted to work on the land and girls wanted to go into domestic service. Most work required only manual skills. Parents felt that farming was learned by experience, not in the classroom. The standard of education was, therefore, poor, with children not interested and parents not caring. This made it difficult to adapt to the changes that were around the corner. Few of these jobs exist today, especially for the women.

Today education has brought many changes but the economy of West Somerset is still based on industries that do not require high qualifications or skills. Although work in tourism has replaced much work in the land-based industries, hours are still long and wages low. However, expectations are higher and people are more dissatisfied with local life. Although unemployment has often been lower than in other places and the quality of life higher, the combination of high cost of living and low wages has meant that the standard of living has been lower. Many have gone off to seek their fortunes whilst others who have made their fortunes have moved in. At present unemployment is falling and the population rising but, in West Somerset at least, the number of jobs has decreased. There are many more retired people now, in particular middle aged people in good health who can afford to retire early. For older and infirm people who cannot drive to the services they need, Exmoor is not the easiest place to live.

Such changes would have happened regardless of whether Exmoor was a National Park. The difference the National Park has made is that they are not as extreme as they would have been. The National Park Authority has worked hard with other organisations to support traditional land-based industries with grants and in the same way has supported tourism and encouraged new industries. It has encouraged tourists to support local services and purchase local produce. Its own work has provided jobs and brought more money into the local economy. Through its planning controls it has also ensured that most new houses built in the National Park are for and affordable by local people. In Luccombe the National Trust has continued a policy of letting its properties to local people, especially those with families and employed locally. In 1992 new houses were built for the West Somerset Housing Association to enable elderly people to stay in the village. They not only provided affordable housing but also reflected local design, winning an award in the process. In the 1940s rural depopulation was setting in and many of the old cottages in the centre of the village had disappeared. Families are smaller now and the same number of people requires more houses.

Whilst services have declined in most rural areas, those in Luccombe and the National Park as a whole have fared better. In the 1940s Luccombe people were more isolated than they are now. People helped each other with buying and distribution of goods. Today many goods can be delivered, although this may be at a cost. There was a new hotel at Wootton Courtenay but Luccombe men drank at Porlock. Today they can drink at Allerford, which is not as far as either. The roads were narrow and still are, but they are better maintained and the nearby A39 is fast and much improved. The parish room was a rarely used 'hut' and the villagers now have a well-equipped building. There was no bus service and now there is a regular service through the village. Telecommunications have improved enormously. The Post Office at Allerford still survives. The nearest doctor was in Porlock and a guinea was charged for a call-out, so he was little used. There is still a doctor in Porlock but the call-out

New houses in Luccombe, early 1990s.

Brian Pearce

is now free. Although few had cars, most shopped in Minehead, where there was a bigger selection than in Porlock. Most now have cars and most still shop in Minehead, although there is a good selection in Porlock. A few went to the cinema or dances in Minehead, where now there are even more entertainment and leisure facilities.

The court house is now nearer but the police station slightly further away. The main change for the worse has been the loss of the local school, although there is a good new school in Porlock and school transport is laid on. It was considered too far for children to walk for the bus in winter and this prevented many from taking secondary education in Minehead. Secondary school is still at Minehead but there is plenty of school transport and free education for all whereas then the Grammar School was fee paying. So there has been change but it has not all been bad and the National Park Authority has done what it can to retain local services.

The village school at Luccombe has now been converted to a parish hall and the old wooden hut has been demolished. Picture taken in the late 1990s.   Brian Pearce

FORESTRY FIRST

AT the public enquiry in 1954 the Inspector said that Exmoor may have few pressures but it was fortunate in this and it was unlikely that it would escape the pressures that were affecting the rest of the countryside. Change was happening, even in Luccombe, but it was relatively slow and barely noticed by people living there. One of the changes the Inspector noted was afforestation. First World War blockades of shipping had shown that the country could not survive for long without imports of timber. During that war old Exmoor broadleaved woodlands were felled for pit props and useful timber was fast running out. Francis Acland had long been an advocate of forestry and headed a committee that put forward proposals for the Forestry Commission, which was established in 1919 to help make Britain more self-sufficient in timber. He became one of the first Forestry Commissioners and set an example by planting up parts of the Holnicote Estate with conifer plantations and mixed woodland. It is clear from the list of workmen in *Exmoor Village* that this contributed to employment on the estate but local forestry has never been very labour intensive and has not compensated the falling number of jobs in agriculture. After the Second World War planting developed more rapidly and forestry seriously threatened the character of Exmoor, especially in the east.

The first big issue for the National Park Authorities to tackle was Forestry Commission proposals to plant the Chains and Furzehill Common with conifers, along with parts of the Heddon Valley. The Authorities had no power to prevent this but were consulted on the proposals. They agreed not to object to the Heddon Valley proposals, providing there was no planting above the 700ft contour and archaeological sites were protected, but objected to the Chains proposal on landscape grounds. The Chains proposal was held up because the Forestry Commission had not yet purchased the land from the owners, Lord and

Forestry on the Holnicote Estate in the 1970s. Exmoor's sheltered combes provide conditions for rapid growth of conifers.

ENPA

Lady Fortescue, when they died in 1958. By the end of the year plans were dropped, partly because of economics and partly because of the strong opposition. Somerset County Council continued to oppose further proposals on the Fortescue Estate to afforest Trout Hill, Kittuck, Warren Cleave, Cornham and Flexbarrow, whilst agreeing to smaller planting at Bale Water, Lime Combe, Halscombe, Ash Combe and Birch Cleave.

Within two years of the setting up of the National Park Authorities the major threat of afforestation had receded. The Authorities had no special powers over land use and conservation efforts were directed through voluntary agreements. They had the idea of working with forestry organisations to draw up maps showing where afforestation would and would not be acceptable. Agreement was soon made between the Authorities, Forestry Commission and the National Parks Commission, which urged all National Park Authorities to adopt this Exmoor precedent. It was not until 1971, however, that a formal agreement was drawn up securing the same degree of consultation with private timber growers as was already operating with the Forestry Commission. A map was drawn up showing where forest plantations existed, where new ones would be acceptable and where they would not be acceptable.

Young volunteers tree planting with Jim Collins, Head Warden, mid 1970s.

ENPA

Exmoor was fortunate in having a forester and landscape architect on its staff who could attempt to resolve differences between amenity and economics and reduce the scenic impact of plantations. Roger Miles was a forestry design expert and his book 'Forestry in the English Landscape' was published in 1967. Exmoor had been pioneering in its voluntary agreements on forestry planting and design and the book showed many examples of its good practice. Other parts of Britain were much less fortunate in having great blocks and rows of conifers imposed unsympathetically on the landscape.

The protection of remaining fragments of ancient woodland proved a more difficult task but crucial to the survival to many species of wildlife. In the 1960s both County Councils were using Tree Preservation Orders to protect large blocks of old oak woodlands for their amenity value. Of particular concern was the replanting of broadleaved woodland with conifers. There was a proposal to gradually fell Burridge Wood at Dulverton, now a Site of Special Scientific Interest, and replant with conifers and beech. The County Councils drew up a list of the traditional

Dave Wood, Forester, gets to grips with the Rhododendron problem on North Hill in the late 1980s. The introduced species Rhododendron ponticum prevents regeneration of trees in many of Exmoor's woodlands.

ENPA

Jonathan Waterer uses his heavy horses to extract cut timber from Hawkcombe Woods to reduce the damage that would have been caused to the ground flora by machinery, late 1980s.

Brian Pearce

woodlands which they felt required greatest protection. These included well known woods at Woody Bay, Heddon Valley, Watersmeet, Culbone, Simonsbath, Badgworthy, Dulverton and Dunster. They pressed the Government for legislation, hoping that a General Powers Bill would give them powers to control afforestation and create special byelaws in National Parks. In 1962 Devon County Council made Tree Preservation Orders on the Heddon Valley, Woody Bay and Watersmeet woodlands. The Heddon Valley woods were subsequently put up for sale. The vendors gave the National Trust the option to buy them and the Trust joined the Exmoor Society in an appeal to raise the money, much of which came from the County Council.

Somerset County Council's first substantial purchase came soon after, when it bought 605 acres of North Hill at Minehead. The purchase was made during voluntary consultation under the Afforestation Agreement. The Economic Forestry Group was proposing major planting on the hill which would have obscured views, restricted public access and destroyed rare heathland. The company suggested that they would ameliorate the proposal by encouraging the spread of sycamore on the remainder of the property. Sycamore, which is broadleaved but not a native tree, is now a great problem in the area.

The Forestry Commission objected to some of the Tree Preservation Orders on the grounds that the woodlands could have a value for timber. 213 acres of Hawkcombe and Colescombe Woods near Porlock had been given a Tree Preservation Order and, because it had proved impossible to reconcile the aims of forestry and conservation, the woodland was purchased by the Somerset County Council in 1965. The National Park Authority continues to purchase woodlands for conservation purposes. Its latest purchase, Tarr Steps woodlands, was made in 2001 with support from the Heritage Lottery Fund. The woodlands have a high value for conservation and public access and have been designated as a National Nature Reserve as part of the Golden Anniversary celebrations.

Later, many areas of woodland that were important for wildlife gained greater protection as Sites of Special Scientific Interest. Under Section 3 of the Wildlife and Countryside Act, 1985 the National Park Authority drew up a map of the woodlands within the National Park, showing which areas were important to be conserved. As part of the survey work the Authority grant aided Somerset and Devon Trusts for Nature Conservation to undertake woodland surveys. Under the Act landowners were obliged to notify the Authority of proposed changes to areas earmarked on the map. Large scale felling also required licences from the Forestry Commission, which was required to consult with the National Park Authority on proposals.

The Government eventually strengthened Tree Preservation Orders to allow for the planting and maintenance of woodlands covered by them. Following these changes, Somerset County Council leased a small plot of land from the National Trust at Allerford to act as a nursery. Trees were raised there to supply the growing amount of woodland in ownership of the National Park Authorities and standard trees were grown up for planting in car parks and picnic sites. Later, many beech saplings were grown for the beech hedgebank scheme introduced by the Authority in 1978. The nursery was worked by a variety of estate staff on a rota basis.

Amid local criticism that the National Park Authority was using ratepayers' money, it started to become more self-sufficient in its own timber. It even managed to sell timber and create employment, not only through its own staffing but also by allowing private businesses to extract timber as part of management of its woodland. More and more time and money was being spent taking timber from Authority wood-lands to a local sawmill. So, in 1980, when the opportunity arose to purchase a suitable bandsaw, it was taken. The saw was installed in a Dutch barn on the Glenthorne estate, close to the Authority's coastal woods and where it would cause minimum disturbance. It was put to good use for many years, processing timber from sustainably managed woodlands for footpath furniture and other public amenities.

With the aim of replacing the sawmill at Glenthorne, the National Park Authority purchased Simonsbath Sawmill and surrounding meadows from the Fortescue Estate in 1996. It safeguarded the buildings from further deterioration and sponsored a survey of the contents, which included machinery and hardware required for carpentry on the Fortescue Estate around forty years before. It also created a footpath across the meadows alongside the leat that formerly supplied the mill's water turbine. Further funding in 1998 enabled the Authority to restore the leat, turbine and buildings. The necessary licences were obtained and the scheme was completed in 2003, when water ran through the leat for the first time in over fifty years. The scheme not only restored a building that illustrated a century and a half of Exmoor's history, it provided a more sustainable means of processing timber through the use of renew-able energy.

The National Park Authority has worked closely with organisations and individuals on forestry matters and has encouraged and helped to

Ash trees growing at the National Park Authority's nursery at Allerford in the 1970s.

ENPA

At work in Yenworthy sawmill, mid 1980s.

ENPA

Stan Curtis, Honorary Warden, demonstrates the restored saw-bench at Simonsbath Sawmill, early 2000s.

ENPA

devise management plans and forest design schemes and provided advice on grants. In December 1981 a hurricane and blizzard caused extensive damage to trees and buildings in the National Park. Winds reached well in excess of 100mph and large areas of woodlands were completely flattened. Worst affected were woods on the Heddon Valley and Lee Abbey estates. The Authority worked with the landowners to clear debris and develop plans for replanting.

With European funding, the Greater Exmoor LEADER Woodland Project commenced in 1998. Its aims were: to encourage farmers and landowners to bring woodlands into positive management, to develop opportunities for employment in woodland management and to organise the provision of training. This work has continued under the 'Woodcert' scheme. The year also saw the start of funding under the Woodland Challenge Fund, a joint initiative between the Association of National Park Authorities and the Forestry Commission. The funds were used as 'top up' grants in addition to the standard Woodland Grant Scheme and Farm Woodland Premium Scheme payments. The extra funds were needed for necessary parts of projects such as land purchase, design, survey, fencing, ground preparation and management planning. The Authority continues not just to administer its own woodlands but to provide grants and advice on grant schemes and encourage the sustainable use of local woodlands both for conservation purposes and employment.

Aerial view of the National Park Authority's woodland at Birch Cleave, Simonsbath, after a gale in the late 1980s.

ENPA

MOOR OR LESS?

XMOOR *Village* mentions farmers being encouraged to plough up moorland during the war, as had occurred in other wars. Luccombe farmers were, however, sceptical about the viability of moorland reclamation. Even though the War Agricultural Committee bought the necessary equipment for them, they thought reclamation was for the larger, wealthier landowners. Reclamation had always taken place, it was just that they were used to the poorer times of the 1920s and 30s. To the residents of Luccombe the moorland seemed endless but they were lucky that their local moorland on Dunkery was protected by the National Trust. Exmoor was one of the few relatively wild, open and tranquil areas remaining in southern England and the loss of its moorland threatened the concept of National Parks as a national resource. Each time a piece of moorland disappeared these qualities were diminished.

Land improvement grants came in with the 1947 Agriculture Act and between 1934 and 1957 about 10,000 acres of Exmoor's moorland disappeared under the plough. By the early 1960s the National Park Authorities were already worried about ploughing and fencing of moorland when a proposal came for ploughing scenic Countisbury Common, along the A39. Whilst compulsory purchase was possible if access was threatened, there was nothing they could do in this case. They tried to persuade the Minister for Housing and Local Government to bring the fencing under planning control, but he refused and so began a long battle to protect Exmoor's moorland. The Authorities pressed the National Parks Commission, who pressed the Government, for powers to do this. The Government made it necessary for farmers to consult the relevant Authority before a ploughing grant was approved but, as in the case of Fyldon Common, they did not always do so. There were no Government grants to compensate farmers for not ploughing moorland and the Authorities set up their own contingency fund.

Heathland on Winsford Hill in the 1950s.

ENPA

Lype Common in 1972, not long after fencing, ploughing and planting of conifers. The remaining heathland soon followed.

ENPA

In 1963 the Exmoor Society commissioned the Second Land Utilisation Survey to carry out a survey of Exmoor to show how the moorland was disappearing. There was much divergence of opinion as to what constituted moorland but it was finally agreed with farmers and landowners that about 6,000 acres of moor and heath had been improved over the period of 1957-67. The National Park Authorities commissioned the Society to produce a map showing the areas of Exmoor which were still in their 'natural state' so that they could decide which of the remaining areas should be protected. The agreed map showed 43,567 acres or 26% of the National Park that was considered critical to the character of the Park. Only 9,934 acres of this had any protection, mostly through ownership by the National Trust.

Whilst they continued to press for legislation, the National Park Authorities formed a Working Group with the landowner's organisations to devise methods of protecting the 'critical' areas of moorland. The result was some 'trade off' agreements, such as on South Hill near Dulverton, whereby less important moorland was sacrificed to save 'critical' areas. It took many years for stronger legislation to be passed, during which time much moorland was lost. The turning point came in

Leonard Curtis: National Park Officer 1978-1988. On retirement he was awarded the OBE for his services to Exmoor.

ENPA

Glenthorne Estate, infra-red aerial photograph from the late 1970s.

ENPA

1977 over the ploughing of Stowey Allotment, part of the moorland 'core'. Despite attempts at purchase, the National Park Authority was unable to prevent reclamation. The resulting political upheaval caused the Environment Minister to appoint Lord Porchester to undertake his 'Study of Exmoor'. His report gave impetus for compensation payments. It also gave rise to the Porchester Maps, which were similar to the Critical Amenity Map in showing the moorland that was considered most important to protect.

Dr Leonard Curtis became Exmoor's second National Park Officer when he took over from Maj Gen Dare Wilson in 1978. He was an expert on soil survey and remote sensing and brought these skills at a time when mapping and monitoring of moorland vegetation became a priority for the National Park Authority. Lord Porchester's definition of moorland was in part based on types of soils. Experiments took place using radar and satellite images to assist in the process of mapping moor and heath. Most useful, however, proved to be aerial photography using infra red film, which shows up vegetation differences. The whole of the National Park was covered by such photography in 1978 and subsequently a quarter of the National Park has been flown each year so that changes can be measured over a four-yearly cycle. The first Porchester Map, showing the extent of moor and heath on Exmoor, was published in 1979 and the second Map, showing those parts of Exmoor's moor and heath that it was particularly important to conserve, came two years later.

Meanwhile, the National Park Authority was making use of the Government's offer of compensatory grants by negotiating a management agreement with the owner of the Glenthorne Estate. Whilst negotiations were under way, it entered two conservation agreements with other farmers. Under conservation agreements payment was in kind. The farmers agreed not to plough or fence their moorland and to control the growth of bracken, gorse and rushes to the benefit of other moorland vegetation. In return National Park staff removed eyesores, planted trees and restored beech hedgerows. The effects of different land treatments and stocking rates were studied to work out the best form of management both for farming and wildlife. In 1979, after three years of negotiations, the Glenthorne management agreement was concluded. This voluntary agreement, which included compensation for the loss of potential income due to conservation measures, was the first of its kind anywhere

Alan Collins, seasonal Warden for the Glenthorne Estate in the early 1980s.

ENPA

and a model for compensatory agreements ever since. Under the agreement some heathland was ploughed and in return the estate was opened up to the public with many new footpaths and a nature trail being made whilst the existing network of Rights of Way was rationalised. Conservation work on the estate became the responsibility of the National Park Authority, including control of hundreds of acres of rhododendrons, and a seasonal Warden was appointed.

Three years after the publication of Lord Porchester's report, a review was undertaken of the effectiveness of its proposals. Over the three years 1,536 acres had been subject to agricultural and afforestation proposals. Of this, 1,017 acres had been protected through management agreements, 230 acres had been ploughed with agreement and 66 acres ploughed without agreement. The Government offered financial support to the Authorities to make such agreements and Exmoor National Park Authority published guidelines for compensation. These laid out principles for independent assessment of the amount of compensation given to farmers for loss of potential income due to conservation measures. The guidelines were tested by a new agreement on Halscombe Allotment, Old Barrow Down and Hawkridge Plain. Under the agreement ploughing was resisted but partial improvement by dressing with lime and slag was allowed. The area was carefully monitored for several years and the agreement was used to show how areas could be improved for both farming and wildlife.

Management agreements were a step forward but not ideal. They could not be enforced, were only temporary and were costly in the long term. Public ownership was still the best protection for moorland.

Aerial view of Warren Farm in the mid 1980s.

ENPA

Several purchases have been made by the National Park Authority since 1962, when North Hill was bought to protect its heathland from afforestation. A much larger purchase was the Chains, Pinkery and Hoaroak Herding in 1970. When the Fortescue Estate's Exmoor holdings were sold off, to secure good prices, moorland areas were offered with plans for agricultural improvements. In the case of Larkbarrow, the Department for the Environment stepped in and purchased the land. By the time Warren came up for sale the National Heritage Fund could be used to purchase the moorland. This had become almost exclusively Molinia grass and purchase allowed the National Park Authority to manage the moorland to increase diversity and allow public access. The farm buildings and in-bye land were sold on with restrictive covenants and an arrangement was made with the new farmer to manage a pony herd and assist with fire prevention. Further large purchases, known as the Exmoor Forest Moorlands, were made from the Fortescue estate with assistance from the fund

The National Park Authority does not have compulsory purchase powers over moorland except where access is threatened and such powers have never been used. Voluntary agreements have always been sought. Most of the high parts of Exmoor form permanent pasture for sheep and cattle and agreements have been based on loss of potential profits from stock rearing. In 1985, encouraged by subsidies, a North Devon farmer was growing crops under an arable rotation that included wheat and rye up to a height of 400 metres above sea level in wet and exposed conditions. Cereals were making high guaranteed prices and a year later he commenced subsoiling moorland at Long Holcombe for cereal production. The National Park Authority did not have any power to prevent reclamation except by recommending that grants should not be given. In this case the potential short term profits were so great and compensation so low that the landowner was prepared to proceed without grants. The issue put much of Exmoor's remaining privately owned moorland under threat and the Authority had to buy the land at an inflated value to prevent reclamation.

Nowadays such direct threats to moorland have receded. In 1989 the National Park Authority published its Section 3 Conservation Map, replacing Porchester Map 2. The Porchester Map showed the areas of moor and heath considered most important to protect and was unique to Exmoor. Under Section 3 of the Wildlife and Countryside Act all National Park Authorities had to produce maps, not just of moor and heath but also of woodland, cliff and foreshore. Publication of the map involved a long consultation process. Following that, English Nature designated

Exmoor's prairies: stubble burning near Long Holcombe in the mid 1980s.

Brian Pearce

David Boyce, Ecologist, talks to children about moorland insects at an open day at Exmoor House, mid 1990s.

ENPA

much of Exmoor's moor and heath as Sites of Special Scientific Interest. This gave legal protection which had not previously existed on such areas. The protection was strengthened by the 1995 Environment Act, as there were many ways in which the value of these areas for wildlife was diminishing other than by reclamation. It was not until 2002 that English Nature undertook surveys of the condition of such sites on Exmoor. About two thirds of the area of such sites was found to be in 'unfavourable' condition for wildlife.

One of the most useful indicators of the condition of moorland is the numbers and variety of moorland birds. In 1963 the National Park Authority looked into the problem of declining numbers of black grouse on Exmoor. From hundreds or even thousands of birds in the 19th century they had disappeared from strongholds because of moorland reclamation and forestry, and from relatively stable sites such as Dunkery. It was felt that frequent moorland burning and burning into the nesting season was partly responsible for the decline, along with disease. By 1968 the species had become extinct and the Somerset Warden was paid for rearing Scottish black grouse chicks for restocking. Lord Ancaster also raised and released chicks from his estate in Scotland, but none survived. Today the red grouse is also on the verge of extinction on Exmoor and several other moorland species are in decline. The National Park Authority sponsors research into moorland birds to assess what is causing the decline and devise remedies.

A success story is that of the Exmoor pony. At the time of writing of *Exmoor Village* the ponies were at their lowest ebb. Few in Luccombe kept ponies and rustling for meat during the war had decimated those on the moor. In 1980, amid a national campaign by the Exmoor Pony Society to draw attention to the low numbers of Exmoor ponies, the National Park Authority established its own breeding programme. Successful breeding on the Authority's land at Haddon Hill was followed by establishment of another herd on its property at Warren. Despite many ponies going to good homes and other conservation organisations, numbers eventually grew to about 50 and the breeding programme was reduced. There are now probably more Exmoor ponies than there have ever been on Exmoor but there are still few-free ranging ponies on moorland.

Management of the remaining moorland has become one of the main issues for the National Park Authority. In 1995 it set up a Moorland Panel of farmers and interested organisations to discuss how best to manage moorland for both stock grazing and wildlife conservation, to encourage

National Park Authority ponies at a round-up at Warren in the 1980s.

ENPA

research and to disseminate its findings. At the time, there was much concern over damage caused by winter grazing of moorland by cattle. Cattle poaching the ground around feeding areas and vehicles carrying feed were reducing some areas of common land to seas of mud. The answer was to make management agreements with the graziers. In some cases this meant compensation for new cattle sheds for feeding indoors in the winter. The agreements were eventually superseded by Environmentally Sensitive Area agreements but payments resulted in a spate of building of huge, unsightly cattle sheds.

Fires, both deliberate and accidental, can be a major problem for moorland wildlife whilst they can also be beneficial. The key lies in control. There were several bad moorland fires in the hot summer of 1976 including what was possibly Exmoor's worst forest fire to date, on Grabbist Hill and Knowle Hill, and fire watching became a major activity for the Wardens. Illegal fires covered over 2,000ha of moorland in the spring of 1997. There was widespread feeling amongst local farmers that too little burning was allowed and the illegal burns had taken place as a result of their frustration. However, the National Park Authority and National Trust operate programmes of controlled burning on their estates and help others with their programmes. Overburning and overgrazing on dry heath favours the spread of bracken. Bracken harbours ticks and illegal burns often take place in attempt to eradicate the ticks, exacerbating the problem. A valuable experiment in bracken control was begun on private land at Bye Common. This showed how spraying could be used to eliminate bracken on steep slopes. The results showed how land could be improved without ploughing and the high input/ high output farming which was of little use for wildlife. Nowadays the National Park Authority is undertaking research into replacing lost moor and heath. This is by no means easy but it is generally easier where heathland has been planted with conifers. The Authority has been experimenting on its own land at Haddon Hill. Little heathland now remains in the Brendon Hills and it is hoped that adjoining heathland will spread back over the site, although results so far have been mixed.

ENJOYMENT AND UNDERSTANDING

IN *Exmoor Village* nobody went abroad for their holidays – if they went on holiday at all it was mostly to towns in southern England. In return, people from those towns were coming to Exmoor. Amongst the criteria for National Parks were that they should be easily accessible from at least one of the major centres of population in England and Wales and for Exmoor these were Cardiff, Bristol, Rhondda, Swansea, Plymouth and Southampton. In *Exmoor Village* it is clear that visitors were already coming from these places. Increase in car ownership, road improvements and more leisure time after the war meant an increase in tourism and pressures on Exmoor that had not been envisaged when the National Park was created. The numbers of visitors reached a peak around the early 1970s. Since then more have been taking their main holiday abroad and coming to Exmoor for shorter breaks.

The purpose of a National Park is not to attract visitors but to help them to enjoy, understand and appreciate the special qualities of the area. Few come because of Exmoor's status as a National Park but many come because it is kept unspoilt and they are helped to enjoy it. Too many visitors can, however, destroy the qualities for which they are coming. In 1974 Lord Sandford's Committee recommended that recreation in

Tourists at Tarr Steps in the late 1950s.

ENPA

National Parks should be confined to that which left the natural beauty unimpaired. This gave rise to the 'Sandford principle' where, if the two main purposes of National Parks came into conflict, conservation should take precedence over recreation. The report also suggested that the recreation should be 'compatible with the qualities of the parks, among which . . . . a sense of tranquillity and of contact with nature seems to us to be of especial value.'

On Exmoor tourism was not seen as a problem and it has been one of the least visited National Parks. Visitors were generally welcomed and they never quite overwhelmed the area. They were treated as friends and often became friends. Accommodation providers relied on word of mouth and repeat custom and most visitors to Exmoor are still repeat customers: 91% of day visitors and 74% of staying visitors have been before. Most Luccombe women let rooms and it was useful pocket money or the main income of some. Today tourism has become Exmoor's main industry but Luccombe has not become devoted to it like some villages. Attitudes vary but most locals accept tourism because they have always known it and, directly or indirectly, their living may depend on it. Indeed, in 1983 when the so-called 'Beast of Exmoor' hit the national headlines the National Park Authority tried to play down the publicity as they thought that it would deter visitors. The foot and mouth crisis in 2001 was also a huge worry. Even though there were no outbreaks in the National Park, few on Exmoor were not affected. It was suggested that tourism was losing five times as much income as farming. The Authority helped by providing a foot and mouth 'hotline' and advisory leaflets.

Luckily the National Park Authority had already set up tourism partnerships which helped to deal with the aftermath of the crisis, improving access to information, promoting local events and developing targeted

Riders at Gallox Bridge, Dunster in the late 1950s.

ENPA

'Exmoor is Open' celebration at Dunkery Gate after the foot and mouth crisis in 2001.

Brian Pearce

marketing. From 1980 it had provided annual seminars for tourist providers and from 1985 it worked with tourism bodies to pioneer the Exmoor Tourism Development Action Programme, which was later copied throughout the country. This attempted to promote tourism based on the character of Exmoor, improve the quality of visitor facilities and the environment and obtain grants for these purposes. This role has been taken on by the Exmoor Tourism Advisory Group, Exmoor Tourism Consortium and now Visit Exmoor. During the 1990s the Greater Exmoor LEADER Project brought European funding for a Tourism Development Worker, leaflets and guides such as the Accessible Exmoor guide for disabled people and for lasting projects such as the Snowdrop Valley park and ride scheme.

From the outset the National Park Authority devised annual programmes of 'positive works' for visitors which would attract grants. The first works were mainly providing lay-bys with viewpoints.

In 1962 grants became available for the purchase of land and buildings and within a couple of years the Authority had provided car parks and picnic areas at Pittcombe Head, County Gate and Tarr Steps. The 1968 Countryside Act allowed the Authority to provide toilets and chemical toilets were added at Tarr Steps but these became a source of complaints until expensive water supply and sewage treatment facilities were added. Today the Authority provides many facilities and most visitors

New layby for motorists to view Dunkery from near Wheddon Cross, late 1960s.

ENPA

The newly-created car park and toilets at Tarr Steps in the late 1960s. The landscaping has now matured and the car park is partly hidden by trees.

ENPA

are contented. It is estimated that half of all the visitors to Exmoor are merely passing through, taking the scenic route to somewhere else and just stopping to use such facilities. Nowadays, however, motoring for leisure is not encouraged and emphasis is on sustainable ways of getting around, such as walking, cycling or public transport.

The Authority can secure accommodation for visitors and it has worked with the Youth Hostels Association to provide a hostel and camping barns. When Somerset County Council bought the Chains and Hoaroak Herding in 1969 its Planning Department leased land at Pinkery to its Education Department for a schools camp site. Work soon began on converting the semi-derelict farmhouse there into an outdoor education centre and courses were provided for pupils and teachers.

In 1994 the lease was given up and the Authority took the centre in hand, helping it diversify and increase income to pay for running costs. Pinkery was to become a 'centre of excellence' in its education programmes, domestic provision, health and safety provisions, and sustainability. The latter has come through recycling and the use of renewable energy, in the form of a wind generator and a photo-voltaic roof which turns sunlight into electricity.

In 1975 Exmoor became one of the first National Park Authorities to appoint a Youth and Schools Liaison Officer. Along with the Wardens, he would provide safety advice and meet groups during their visits. During 'Adventure Weeks' at Butlins at Minehead they advised up to up to a thousand teachers at a time and supervised walks with up to 1,500

The car park and toilets at Tarr Steps, 2004

Heather Lowther

Dave Gurnett, Education Ranger, works with children at a Woodland Crafts Week in Hawkcombe Woods, mid 1990s.

ENPA

The National Park Information Centre at Minehead in the early 1970s.

ENPA

people per walk. Hundreds of thousands of children have now benefited from the education services provided. Today there is an education team with emphasis on working on projects with local schools and most Exmoor children have some contact with National Park staff.

Early grants were mostly for capital projects. From the early 1960s Government money could also be used for staff but it was not until after local government reorganisation in 1974 that there was any more than a handful of employees. The first National Park Information Centre was opened in the former library building at Minehead in 1962, Mr Strickland, the Publicity Officer, becoming the first member of National Park staff. He covered all aspects of information and publicity, taking displays to shows, museums and even Butlin's.

In 1968 Ron 'Skippy' Skipworth became Devon Warden, spending his summer months running a mobile information centre on the sea front at Combe Martin and taking it to shows. When the Authority opened its offices at Dulverton it used a room as an information centre, manned by volunteer staff and locals.

David Potter, Forward Planning Officer, volunteers to man the Information Centre at Exmoor House, late 1970s.

ENPA

Other centres have been developed as the opportunity has arisen, in places where visitors congregate. Relocating the Lynmouth Visitor Centre in 1982 made it one of the busiest Visitor Centres in the West Country, topping 200,000 customers a year. Plans for one large, purpose-built centre at County Gate were rejected on the basis that it was better to spread facilities as widely as possible. Following this a scheme to support village shops was introduced, whereby shops became 'Local Information Points' for both visitors and the local community. In 1998 The Authority opened its web site, with emphasis placed on information being easy to locate and download and enabling the public to communicate with the Authority more easily. Information points with internet access are following.

The first National Park Wardens started work in 1963 – the Devon Warden, Major W R Clarke, in April and Somerset Warden, Commander Jim Collins, in June, on starting salaries of just £710 per annum. Their grants limited what they could do and they overcame this by using voluntary help to clear litter, maintain paths and remove eyesores. Much of the Wardens' time was taken up maintaining paths. The Somerset Warden took up the offer of a grant to pilot a scheme of waymarking some walks. The Dunster area became the first in Britain to have such walks and the scheme was expanded to cover the Somerset side of Exmoor. Devon County Council was against waymarking because it was considered to be intrusive, particularly on open moorland, and also because it did not fulfil the public's wish for circular routes. A unified approach came after 1974 and in 1993 Exmoor's waymarks were repainted under a national system, using colours to denote the status of routes.

A bonus of the original scheme was the development of 'permissive' paths. Many landowners were happy to provide substitute paths where the use of legal Rights of Way caused problems, such as where they ran through farmyards. The 1968 Countryside Act put a huge burden on local authorities to signpost Public Rights of Way from roads and contribute towards the costs of gates and stiles on them. The timber for these and the signs is generally produced sustainably from the conservation management of the Authority's own woodlands and they are made in its workshop at Exford.

In *Exmoor Village* locals were not concerned about access for walking as they had little leisure time. Landowners would grant access to moors in the summer for women and children to pick whortleberries. Stag, fox or otter hunting with hounds was the main leisure pursuit and locals

Mary Beasley, Information Assistant, demonstrates a new 'out of hours' information facility at Lynmouth National Park Information Centre, late 1980s.

ENPA

Jim Collins, Head Warden, adds National Trail waymarks to Coast Path signs on North Hill in the mid 1970s.

ENPA

Painting the characteristic hand-routed footpath signs at the workshop at Cutcombe in the mid 1970s. The signs are made of oak from the conservation management of the National Park authority's woodlands.

ENPA

could generally follow the hunts where they liked. Apart from rough shooting, there was no grouse shooting on the moors and people were not kept away like they were in northern National Parks. However, they were not encouraged either, as landowners were concerned about liability. Sir Thomas (Charlie) Acland had opened up much of his estate to the public and provided paths and rides but visitors generally had no idea where they were allowed to walk. It was not until the 1949 National Parks and Access to the Countryside Act that definitive maps of Rights of Way were drawn up. Access to open country was mostly secured through public ownership. From 2000 the National Park Authority became an 'access authority', allowing it to make and enforce such access over private land. A Local Access Forum of interested groups was created to sort out problems, including damage to property. Exmoor has not suffered greatly from erosion by walkers but in 1993 the National Trust restored the summit of Dunkery Beacon after survey showed that Exmoor's highest point had been worn down by nearly 3ft since they acquired it. The Trust and National Park Authority formed a partnership - the Dunkery Project – to combat further erosion. Learning from other National Parks, they developed their own cheap and effective subsoiling technique for repairing eroded paths. Having restored 30km of paths on Dunkery, the project was extended as the Exmoor Paths Partnership with European funding and new partners, including local tourist providers. The scheme was successful in developing 'visitor payback' initiatives

The Exmoor Paths Patrnership team restoring paths on Dunkery, late 1990s.

ENPA

whereby donations from visitors went directly to path maintenance.

The idea for a Long Distance Footpath along the Exmoor coast was mooted well before Exmoor became a National Park. Negotiations with landowners took many years and some sections were not possible until purchase by the National Trust under Enterprise Neptune in the 1960s. The Exmoor section of the South West Coast Path was finally opened in 1975. Despite special grants, maintenance of the path has been a cause of concern for the Authority, with frequent landslips requiring the path to be rerouted. The South West Coast Path project was later set up to survey the use and condition of the path and draw up a strategy for its long-term care and promotion. Plans for the 'Two Moors Way' as a National Bridleway were dropped but in 1976 the route was opened as a footpath and in 1987 Devon County Council opened the Tarka Trail, another long-distance route linking Exmoor and Dartmoor. The project was an early attempt at sustainable tourism - encouraging recreation based on quiet country pursuits.

A regular programme of talks and events for locals and visitors has run since 1965 and over a hundred people turned up for some of the 'Walk with a Warden' walks in the 1970s. Many came without suitable clothing and with complete ignorance of the countryside. Cattle, and bulls in particular, were the main reason cited why they would not go for

Arnold Whincup, Forester, surveys a landslip on the South West Coast Path in Culbone Woods in the late 1970s.

ENPA

Terry Robinson, Interpretation Officer, and Alan Dudden, Area Warden, lead a guided walk in the mid 1970s.

ENPA

George Eamer, Technician, installs an information board at Tarr Steps car park in the mid 1980s.

ENPA

a walk on their own. In the 21st century, with emphasis more on themed events than general walks, they are as popular as ever.

In the late 1960s the Somerset Authority worked with the Somerset Trust for Nature Conservation to set up the first self guided walks in the National Park – one on North Hill and one at Cloutsham. At the same time it installed the first information boards. In 1976 the Countryside Commission seconded an officer to work with the Authority for three years to produce the first Interpretive Plan for a National Park and a model for other authorities. It identified the special features of Exmoor along with opportunities for action for all organisations concerned with helping the public to understand them.

To answer the demand for information from the tourist industry, work began on an official guidebook in 1959 and from then onwards a range of leaflets and booklets has been produced by the National Park Authority. The Exmoor Visitor newspaper was launched in 1984, using advertising to subsidise its free circulation. It is now seen by two thirds of all visitors to Exmoor. In 1990 the Authority went into partnership with a private publisher to produce books under the Exmoor Books label. The aim of the partnership has been to produce books about Exmoor which would not otherwise find a publisher and this book is one of many successful results.

Steven Pugsley and Lady Gass, Chairman of Exmoor National Park Authority, launch another Exmoor Books title with local author, Hope Bourne (centre).

ENPA

THE BEST LAID PLANS

EOPLE in *Exmoor Village* would not have been concerned about planning regulations as there was little development control, despite new housing. Development was swallowing up 25,000ha of countryside around English towns each year. From the early 1930s County Councils had powers to control development in special areas but these were not exercised on Exmoor. The spate of reconstruction after the war led to the general introduction of planning regulations. From 1944 developers were encouraged to consult County Councils and three years later this became a legal requirement.

Between 1957 and 1974 the National Park was run by the planning departments of the two County Councils. The Councils covered both planning policy and day to day planning applications, the National Parks Commission being consulted on major developments, on which the Government had the final say. From 1974 the National Park Authority under Somerset County Council had its own planning section and from 1997 the Authority became a local planning authority in its own right. It never had the draconian powers to control development that many assumed. Planning procedures were much the same as elsewhere except that the minimum size of development for which planning permission was required was slightly lower. Stronger legislation came in 1989, under which any domestic building bigger than the average garden shed required planning permission, along with changes to existing buildings such as stone cladding and dormer windows. The Hobhouse Report had singled out corrugated iron farm buildings as being a particular problem but it was not until 1986 that Government gave powers to National Park Authorities to bring the design, materials and siting of new farm buildings and roads under a limited form of planning control. Even today, however, there are no separate rules as to what can or cannot be built in a National Park. Applications are determined on the basis of law, policies in local development plans and Government guidance.

Members of the Planning Committee on a site visit to decide on an application to restore a derelict cottage near Luxborough, mid 1980s.

ENPA

One advantage of living in a National Park is that the planning section is small and the planners are easily accessible and available to give advice. For these reasons a National Park planning advice centre was set up at Lynton Town Hall in 1975. Most planning applications are approved as problems are generally sorted out by negotiation before formal applications are made. Helpful advice came in 1958 when the Somerset Sub-committee's booklet 'Building on Exmoor' became the first guide to good design for new buildings in a National Park and was held as an example of good practice to authorities throughout Britain. Exmoor's third design guide has now been produced.

Exmoor has been lucky in that it has not had unsightly large developments such as major roads and power lines that have blighted other National Parks and it remains one of the only National Parks free of mining, quarrying, military bases and heavy industry. Its largest development to date has been a reservoir. From 1967 studies were made of several potential sites within the Exe catchment area resulting in a short list of four sites: Landacre, Wimbleball, Kemps and Hartford. The National Park Authority voiced strong objections to the Landacre site on landscape grounds: Landacre Bridge would have been drowned and Cow Castle made an island. The water and river authorities argued that the Wimbleball site was the cheapest option. The National Park Authority, deciding that it was also the least damaging option, gave approval providing that it was consulted on design and use of the reservoir. Much care was taken in the landscaping of the dam and reservoir, under the guidance of Dame Sylvia Crowe.

In the early 1960s there was a spate of applications for communication masts on Exmoor's skyline. Whilst small masts were often approved in the National Park, Exmoor's tallest masts were erected just outside the

The Haddeo Valley before being flooded by Wimbleball Lake, mid 1970s.

ENPA

Construction of Wimbleball dam in the late 1970s.

ENPA

Artists impression of proposed weather radar at Shoulsbury, mid 1980s.

ENPA

boundary on Brendon Hill. Further pressure came in 1985, with proposals for a weather radar. Developers argued that a high moorland site was essential and an application for a site at Shoulsbury was brought to a public enquiry. The Inspector recommended approval but the Secretary of State for the Environment turned down the proposal on environmental grounds.

In the late 1990s it was mobile telephone masts that confronted National Park planners. Government advice was that such masts should be allowed along main roads and the National Park Authority devised policies so that as much as possible would be done to hide them. One mast at Wheddon Cross was disguised as a tree.

The National Park Authority takes care to consult with local people about their needs. Sometimes, however, it has to differentiate between what is claimed to be a need and what may simply be a desire to develop. Generally, whether inside a National Park or not, development is not allowed away from existing settlements unless it supplies a need for farming, fishing or forestry. There have long been attempts to justify other developments on this basis and in the early 1990s several controversial cases tested planning regulations. In one it was argued that a golf course near Lynton was necessary for farm diversification but the project was uneconomic without further, more intrusive developments. A farm near Exford was sold and the farm buildings converted to holiday

Telecommunications mast (left) disguised as a tree at Wheddon Cross, late 1990s.

ENPA

cottages. The owner then argued that new buildings were needed for the farm and its manager. When the application was approved calls were made to tighten planning law to prevent further occurrences. The National Park Authority also pressed the Government to extend planning regulations to cover fish farms. Such farms had considerable impact on the environment yet many such businesses were not viable, raising concerns that they were being used as an excuse to build houses in the countryside. Concern also arose over attempts by a millionaire to create a country estate around Challacombe. He cleared sixty acres of land for parkland, grubbing out hedgerows, draining bogs, felling trees, building huge farm buildings and developing the estate for shooting. The National Park Authority had little power to prevent such changes, although it could exercise constraint when he started to turn the old farmhouse into a 'grand house', using granite from a demolished French chateau.

What development is allowed in the National Park is based on surveys of local needs and set out in Development Plans. In 1958 Somerset County Council produced the first such plan to include policy for the National Park. Development Plans were later replaced by County Structure Plans, which gave general policy for whole counties, and Area Local Plans, which gave more detail for smaller areas. A park-wide Local Plan is now mandatory. Exmoor's first such plan was completed in 1997. The plan is under continual review and in 2001 the National Park Authority concluded a series of 20 'Planning for Real' events which enabled local people to give their views on issues affecting their communities. About 25% of the National Park's population attended, providing material for the next plan.

Housing has been the biggest issue for most Local Plans. About 10% of Exmoor's housing stock is second homes and this restricts opportunities for local people to buy homes.

In 2001 a stir was caused when the National Park committee pressed for second homes to be classed separately from other dwellings for planning permission. If a permanent dwelling was changed to a part-time dwelling, then planning permission would be required, with the intention of withholding permission for lower price properties which could be used as starter homes for local people. The proposals raised a storm of protest from second home owners and estate agents and were never implemented. However, the Authority added weight to demands for second homes to be charged full Council Tax.

From the 'Planning for Real' exercise, speeding traffic was highlighted as one of the main problems in the National Park. There was considerable

Housing for local people at Brompton Regis, late 1980s.

ENPA

Camping at Bossington in the mid 1960s.
ENPA

debate over the design of traffic control schemes as the necessary signs and constructions were seen to be urbanising the rural environment. Exmoor has traffic problems but they are generally not as bad as in most other parts of southern England. In the early 1970s caravans became a problem, with overloading of official sites and unauthorised overnight parking but fears that new roads would bring increased traffic have generally been unjustified.

When the Avonmouth Bridge on the M5 was opened in 1975 it brought a further 14 million people within 3½ hours driving time of Exmoor but by the time the motorway was complete the popularity of package holidays abroad had increased, as had the network of motorways, making it just as easy for visitors to go elsewhere. Visitors started coming to Exmoor for short breaks and the time they wanted to spend travelling shortened, so they did not come from any further away than before. Twenty years later Exmoor was signposted from the motorway amid concern that there were not enough people coming. Signposting of the North Devon Link Road, constructed in the 1980s took some of the traffic previously crossing the moors, commercial traffic in particular, around the boundary instead.

In *Exmoor Village* few villagers had access to a car although some would hire a car or taxi for special occasions. The nearest bus stop was a mile and a half away and that restricted movement, particularly for the elderly and infirm, and discouraged children from taking secondary education in Minehead.

Now buses come right into the village and school transport is available. For a while, however, lack of public transport became more of a problem. Exmoor was never well endowed with railways and the National Park Authorities could do little except protest about closures of local line in the late 1960s and early 1970s.

Promises to replace the services with buses were short lived. The National Park Authority encourages the County Councils to subsidise some rural services, which it helps to promote. From 1976 the Authority sponsored the 'Coastlink' bus service to enable walkers to explore sections of the Coast Path. However, cheap fares, free guided walks and links with the West Somerset Railway were not enough to encourage people to leave their cars behind.

In 1994 the Authority tried to reduce traffic by promoting a circular

The open road: motoring on Exmoor in the 1950s.

ENPA

The demise of Exmoor's railway services: Dulverton Station in the mid 1970s.

ENPA

'... then three come along at once'- Coastlink buses at Kentisbury Ford, late 1970s.

ENPA

service around Exmoor with suggestions for walks which could be undertaken using the service. The services ran for two seasons but the subsidy per passenger was too great for the County Council to bear. An experimental park and ride scheme for the relief of parking problems in Lynmouth met with similar failure. More successful was the service to Wimbleball Lake in the 1980s. A private minibus company took visitors from Dulverton to the lake for guided walks whilst bringing back residents of outlying villages for shopping. The use of the service by visitors kept the subsidy per passenger low, allowing the service to continue for the locals in the winter. Another successful scheme has been the Snowdrop Valley park and ride scheme. From the 1980s the narrow road at Drapers Way, near Cutcombe became congested with vehicles coming to see the wonderful display of snowdrops in February. Attempts to control traffic and reduce publicity for the site failed until the bus service

Snowdrop Valley park and ride scheme, late 1990s.
ENPA

was introduced in 1997. This was set up with European funding but continued largely self financing with assistance from the National Park Authority.

National Park planning is not just about control of development, it is also about making improvements. In 1961 an unsightly static caravan site in the Valley of Rocks became the Devon Authority's first substantial purchase. This and subsequent purchases at Simonsbath and Blackmoor Gate, enabled the removal of eyesores and creation of amenities such as car parks, toilets and picnic areas.

Since 1967 local planning authorities have been able create Conservation Areas. Within such areas development is more strictly controlled but advantages are brought to residents in the form of improvement grants. The National Park Authorities quickly embarked on a programme of designations but sometimes met fierce individual opposition and negotiations with residents often took several years. Conservation Area status led to enhancement schemes. A scheme at Lynmouth was devised during consultation on the Lynton and Lynmouth Local Plan. It involved turning Lynmouth's main street into a pedestrian area and paving over the road and met with great support from shopkeepers.

As a result of a questionnaire to residents of Porlock concerning potential improvements to their village, many of the overhead wires in the village were laid underground. In 1992 an affordable housing scheme

Blackmoor Gate in the early 1980s. The National Park Authority purchased the site to clear up the clutter of signs, buildings and scrapped cars.
ENPA

Pedestrianisation of Lynmouth's main street came as part of a Conservation Area enhancement scheme, mid 1980s.

Brian Pearce

Consolidation of the ruins of Burrow Farm engine house, late 1980s.

Brian Pearce

within the Conservation Area of Luccombe won a Civic Trust Award for its architecture. The houses were built for the West Somerset Housing Association to enable elderly people to stay in the village. The new houses reflected local design, with white painted rendered walls, steeply pitched tiled roofs, simple timber casement windows and tall corner chimneys. In 1996 the National Park Authority entered a Conservation Areas Partnership with English Heritage. Partnership schemes were identified for improving buildings in Lynton and Lynmouth, Parracombe, Twitchen and certain historic farmsteads. Enhancement also takes place outside of Conservation Areas, including historic buildings such as Burrow Farm Engine House and the winding house and incline on the West Somerset Mineral Railway.

Whilst Development, Structure and Local Plans gave the policies for development within the National Park, plans showing how National Park purposes in general were to be fulfilled were not necessary until the 1972 Local Government Act was passed. Such plans were for everyone concerned with Exmoor – not just the National Park Authority - and there has been widespread public consultation on the four plans produced so far. A problem with such consultation has been that issues such as the agricultural economy, hunting, housing, traffic and transport, which are not primary National Park purposes, tend to be foremost in the minds of locals. The balance between farming, forestry and conservation has been the most controversial aspect of most plans. Nowadays the emphasis is on sustainable development, showing that National Park purposes can be achieved in conjunction with a healthy local economy. The plans, now known as National Park Management Plans, have become more visionary, with detail coming in other plans such as the National Park Authority's Business and Local Plans. Alongside the plan has developed a State of the Park Report, showing how Exmoor is changing and providing facts and figures on which to base future policies.

FARMING AND THE FUTURE

NATIONAL Parks are not museums. Change can and does occur within them, whilst special qualities are protected. The surveyors for *Exmoor Village* admired the quality of light, fresh air, wide open space and tranquillity. Characteristic features such as the deer and magnificent walnut trees on the estate were mentioned, along with the narrow, leafy lanes with few passing places. Such inaccessibility prevented crowds from spoiling the tranquillity and continuity of families gave a sense of permanence to the area's character.

Most people who worked then worked with their hands. The Holnicote Estate employed a mason and grew wheat for thatching, so the skills that kept Luccombe's buildings distinct were kept alive but other skills were disappearing. There were few modern buildings then but many houses were in poor condition and offered few facilities. Modernisation was inevitable and Exmoor's planners have striven to encourage architects to design buildings to be of their age but retain local character. The beautiful churches at Dunster, Selworthy, Porlock and Luccombe that were mentioned in *Exmoor Village* have survived, along with other important buildings such as Dunster Castle and Yarn Market, but few lesser buildings have survived without alteration. The older parts of Exmoor villages would still be recognisable to Luccombe residents of the 1940s, along with most of the countryside and the special qualities are still there to be enjoyed. Luccombe itself is still outwardly much the same in appearance and physical changes have mostly been for the better. It is the people and the way of life that have changed.

National Parks have been a compromise between the needs of locals and the needs of the nation. The changes that have affected Exmoor have mostly been the same as have affected the whole nation but it is local people who have largely made those changes. In the early days of National Parks resources were a key issue and it was thought that National Parks could be protected by the planning system without extra resources from Government. This was why their management was given

Traditional skills – thatching at Porlock Weir in the 1970s.

ENPA

Scenes from the past: dairying at Wheddon Cross in the late 1970s. A combination of fast traffic and low prices for milk put an end to scenes like this.

ENPA

Oat stooks above Oare in the 1970s. Subsidies favoured sheep and beef farming on Exmoor and mixed farming became unusual except around the fringes of the moor.

ENPA

to the County Councils – the local planning authorities. Land use for farming, forestry and fisheries was not under planning control but these have been the chief agents of change in the National Parks. Farming has become more intensive and mechanised and this has brought both changes to the countryside and the community. As farming has become big business the rural working classes have been disappearing and along with them local customs and character. It was assumed that farming was the means of maintaining the landscape and that a prosperous faming industry would sustain the local community. Employment in agriculture, however, has been dropping steadily since the introduction of cheap imported foods at the end of the 19th century.

When the National Park was created farming was generally mixed and operated more like organic farms do today. Most communities had dairy farms which supplied their local needs and most farm animals were traditional local breeds. However, war resulted in a lack of feeding-stuff which meant that much Exmoor stock had to be fattened elsewhere. For the same reason much poultry and pig farming ceased and Exmoor farms began to concentrate on sheep and beef farming. After the war there were food shortages but everyone expected cheap food and in an open market there were more cheap imports from abroad. Agricultural subsidies began in the late 1940s and these allowed intensification of agriculture and reclamation of moorland. Subsidies based on the numbers of farm animals made a huge difference to farming on Exmoor and by the late 1980s the grazing pressure of sheer numbers of animals was having an impact on its wildlife. In a study on Monitoring Landscape Change during the 1970s and 1980s, the changes for Exmoor echoed those of other parts of Britain: loss of moorland, hedgerows and rough pasture; increase in coniferous plantation, bracken and cultivated land.

From the 1970s the National Park Authority was investigating methods of using subsidies for conservation measures and not just to support production. In 1978, in response to its study of beech hedgerows, the Authority launched a pilot scheme to provide grants for their restoration, allowing farmers the difference between the cost of fencing and the cost of laying the hedges and making up the banks. Eventually Government was persuaded to introduce similar grants. The management agreements pioneered by the Authority in the 1970s were a big step forward. The main problem with them was that they were expensive and it was hoped that more money would be available under the Government's Environmentally Sensitive Area (ESA) Scheme introduced in 1987. Farmers in this scheme would be liable for compensation payments for environmentally friendly farming. Exmoor did not become an ESA for six years and, meanwhile, the National Park Authority started its own Farm Conservation Scheme. Under the scheme, participants were paid to maintain the traditional landscape of their farms, with payments geared to the conservation value of the land and other features such as hedgerows and vernacular buildings. About the same time the Authority introduced its Landscape Conservation Grant Scheme, providing funding for countryside management projects not covered by other schemes. Projects included hedge restoration, rhododendron control, fencing of woodlands and revival of orchards.

Many of the suggestions put forward by the Authority were incorporated in the Environmentally Sensitive Area scheme. Land of high conservation value now benefits from payments where farmers undertake to farm in an environmentally sensitive manner. Payments increase for areas of moorland which would benefit from special attention, while a Conservation Plan can earn farmers more for work such as hedge planting, rebuilding walls, renovating buildings or improving moorland for wildlife. Whilst payments are mostly for reducing stocking levels, it is hoped that future payments will be more for positive works rather than simply doing less and that they will favour organic farming and making farms more self reliant, with a return to mixed farming. ESA is just one of a growing list of grant schemes and the National Park Authority's Farm and Countryside Advisory Service scheme offers free advice to farmers and landowners on all matters relating to what have become known as agri-environment schemes. The future of Exmoor as a National Park greatly depends upon such schemes. This, however, means that it is very vulnerable to change from fluctuating economic conditions. The schemes need to be long term to have any effect. So far it is clear that the countryside is being better managed as a result of such schemes but their effect on wildlife has not yet been demonstrated and it is hoped that in the future schemes will be devised to meet biodiversity targets, including restoration of heathland and woodland.

The conservation function of National Parks was originally simply one of conservation of scenery and character. Wildlife, however, has long been seen as an essential part of these. In 1997 the purposes of National Parks were changed to include wildlife conservation. English Nature has given wildlife greater protection to wildlife on Exmoor through the creation of Sites of Special Scientific Interest and National Nature Reserves but this has not necessarily halted the decline of some species. Resources have not been available to manage such areas for conservation or to protect nature in other areas. English Nature and the National Park Authority have worked together to produce a Biodiversity Action Plan for Exmoor, which concentrates on key species and habitats. Little is

Exmoor Horn sheep for sale at Exford Auction Field in the late 1970s. The field, is now a picnic area belonging to Exmoor National Park Authority.

ENPA

Clearing of Hadborough Plantation to restore heathland on Haddon Hill.

ENPA

known of the status and habitat requirements of many species and much of the work of the plan is survey work. Surveys highlight the problems but huge resources are often required to tackle them.

The National Park Authority has sponsored surveys on both the habits of deer and the economics of deer hunting. It has no powers of control in this respect but has concerns about the socio-economic effects of a general hunting ban on Exmoor and has sponsored research on these and on the management of deer. Research on deer movements and feeding habits has been useful in helping to assess the numbers of deer which could be tolerated on Exmoor. Such information may be necessary for alternative methods of control of deer. There is already a forum for deer management on Exmoor but in future there may have to be many local groups involved in the practical management of deer in the National Park and the Authority will have a key coordinating role.

One of the biggest changes affecting wildlife will be climate change. Exmoor contributes little towards this in terms of 'greenhouse gasses' but receives the effects of air pollution from the rest of Britain and the Continent. The National Park Authority alone cannot prevent such changes, it can only hope to manage them. Exmoor would be greatly affected by climate change if the Gulf Stream Drift were to disappear, as well as by sea level rises. In *Exmoor Village* it was mentioned that the shingle ridge at Porlock Weir was building up at the harbour entrance. In 1996 a storm breached the ridge, severing the South West Coast Path and allowing Porlock Marsh to flood with sea water at high tides. Amid calls from Porlock residents and landowners for the breach to be filled, a Porlock Bay and Marsh Working Group of landowners and interested organisations was set up. A survey was conducted and all options considered. A policy of limited intervention was considered the only viable

Erecting the wind generator at Pinkery, late 1990s.

Heather Lowther

one and the one that would least damage the Site of Special Scientific Interest. It involved removing the sluice system on the Marsh and groynes on the beach to allow the natural movement of shingle and draining of the Marsh. It was felt that under this option the breach would be naturally sealed or a saltmarsh would build up, as was already happening.

Regarding climate change, the National Park Authority follows the adage 'think globally, act locally'. It encourages renewable energy schemes and has set examples by reducing energy use in its own buildings, reinstating the water turbine at Simonsbath sawmill and installing wind and solar energy generators at Pinkery. Exmoor was once a leading area for the development of water power and it is hoped that it will continue to do so with the development of a tidal power generator off Lynmouth. Exmoor is unlikely to be covered with wind farms. Even if it were, their contribution to the energy needs of the region would be small. Small scale generators, supplying localised needs are, however, welcomed. Much hope rests on the more efficient use of wood as a fuel. Firewood is produced as a by-product of the conservation management of woodlands and as such is a sustainable fuel. Modern wood chip heaters and boilers are very efficient and cut heating costs. Burning the fuel emits some greenhouse gasses but the replacement trees absorb them. In future it is hoped that there will be planting of woodlands for such purposes.

Under the 1995 Environment Act the socio-economic well-being of the local community became a duty of the National Park Authority. Government funding for the countryside became more focussed on community issues and the aims of National Park Authorities became centred on the delivery of National Park purposes through local communities. Economic development is not a purpose in itself but the aim is for sustainable development which also achieves environmental and social objectives. In 2002, following the downturn in the local economy due to the foot and mouth crisis, the National Park Authority issued a statement on the economy of Exmoor. The statement provided an overview of the economy with a wide range of suggestions and proposals for future action. In 2003 the Government introduced a Sustainable Development Fund which could be administered by National Park Authorities, offering grants for projects supporting National Park purposes.

Exmoor communities have similar disadvantages to those in most rural areas but these are offset by the quality of the environment and the status of the National Park, which attracts people and funding to the area. Improved communications mean people can work from home and Exmoor attracts people who bring small businesses to the area. Demands from people with such businesses will ensure that Exmoor is never too far behind in the use of new technology. However, it also attracts people for retirement. Half of the Exmoor community now is not economically active and, although the population is growing, the trend is towards fewer jobs overall. The remaining economy is becoming more diverse, so communities are becoming more divergent in their interests. Conservation organisations, including the National Park Authority, have brought jobs to the area and will continue to do so. They also create a demand for traditional rural skills and will support training in these so that more local people will be able to remain in the area.

Tourism will probably continue to be the main employer. There may not be great changes in numbers of visitors overall but more will be coming out of the main tourist season. Emphasis is being placed on the quality of the visitor experience. Tourists are becoming more sophisticated, wanting areas to be different in character and local food is making a comeback. Visitors will also have the benefit of new access areas. Most of Exmoor's open countryside will be completely open to walkers. As pressures increase on other parts of the countryside such areas will become more valued and, hopefully, better protected as a result. 'Visitor payback' schemes are currently small scale but increasingly visitors will be paying for the quality of environment they come to enjoy and tourist providers will become more environment friendly in their policies.

The people of *Exmoor Village* could not have predicted the changes that took place in the first 50 years of the National Park and it is not possible to predict the changes that will occur in the next 50 years. National Parks have, however, been test beds for policies which have later been applied to the whole of the countryside. As the countryside becomes smaller it will come to be valued more. The countryside is vulnerable to many outside influences and is bound to change. It is hoped that the changes will be managed in line with the values by which National Parks were created.

APPENDIX I
Contents of two typical Luccombe Bookcases
All appendices aappeared in the original *Exmoor Village* book, published 1947

1

Two Bibles
Two Prayer Books
The Great Book of Humour
Enquire Within upon Everything
Webster's Improved English Dictionary
John of Gerisan, by John Oxenham
Cleopatra, by Rider Haggard
The Case of the Howling Dog, by E.S. Gardner
True Blue, by W.H.G. Kingston
Minehead: a guidebook
Britain under Shellfire, by F. Illingworth
A Modern Circe (published 1890)
Molly Bawn (published 1885)
Sister Teresa, by George Moore
Idols, by W.J. Locke
The Danger Line, by Joan Sutherland
The Womans' Weekly Bedside Book
The Soul of Gold, by Justus Miles Forman
White Fang, by Jack London
Daisy's Aunt, by E.F. Benson
Trooper O'Neil, by George Goodchild
The Light of Scarthey, by Egerton Castle
The Little Man, by John Galsworthy
The Top of the World, by E.M. Dell
My Official Wife, by R.H. Savage
And two or three *Lilliputs, Home Notes,* and *Life*

2

Six volumes of *The Gardener's Assistant*
The Navy in Battle, by Arthur H. Pollen
Lost among the Red Men, by E.S. Ellis
Front Line 1940–41 (Ministry of Information)
Blackie's Boys' Annual
The Jolly Stay Book
Puddings – Proved and Approved
Arnold's *Geography*
Henry Brocken, by Walter de la Mare
Home Truths, by the Rev. J.C. Ryle
The English Gardener (a novel)
Billy Bray, by F.W. Bairne
Prayers for Private Life
The Book of Common Prayer
Two Bibles
District Railway Map of London
Siamese White, by Maurice Collis (Penguin)
Egerton Roscoe: A Story for the High Spirited
My Prayer Book for Women and Girls
The Childrens' Faith, by the Rev. E.W. Osborne
Gulliver's Travels, by Swift
Old Moore's Almanack
The Comparative Atlas
Hymns, Ancient and Modern
Reconciliation, by J.F. Rutherford
The Thread of Gold, by A.C. Benson
The New Royal Readers, Vol. VIII
With the Eagles, by Pearl L. Anderson
The Talisman, Vol. I, by Sir Walter Scott
Nature Caricatures
The Crowning of the King and Queen of England
Daily Mirror Reflections in Wartime (cartoons of the first World War)
Ranks, Medals, and Ribbons (pamphlet of the second World War)
The Abysmal Brute, by Jack London
Four very old paperback novels
Three Cookery books issued by Arnold's "Self-raising Flour"

Furniture

One armchair with flowered chintz cover, flowered chintz cushion, and antimacassar, white with lace edges.

One sofa, flowered chintz, not matching the chair. Two cushions, one blue silk, one green tapestry. Antimacassar.

Five wooden chairs. One with American cloth seat covering, two with yellow cloth, two with red cloth.

Two tables. One near window, round, but with one leaf folded, giving flat surface next to the wall. A bowl of tulips on it. The other near the kitchen door, with both flaps down. On it a wireless and battery, a large yellow china spirit lamp, with flowers painted on it. Photograph of her eldest son, in France.

One sideboard, cheapish and badly finished, and covered with a white runner. On it a biscuit tin, a box of matches, photograph of son (dead), butter dish, saucer, fruit bowl, glass vase with flowers, model galleon, large cruet, serviette rack.

Floor

Light-brown linoleum, with small red and brown patterns.

Three carpets. One very old, faded grey strip towards the door. Mauve and brown patterned one by the hearth. Newish brown and black patterned one near the table.

On the Window-sill

Two pottery jugs.
One plant-stand in the shape of a black cat, with basket for plants attached.
One paperweight, with Chinese figuring.
One ashtray.

On a small Window-ledge

One cactus-plant in a pot.

On the Mantelpiece

In the centre a clock in a wooden case. On the left, from left to right:

- A. Vase, flowered on pink glass. Elaborate fluted top.
- B. Vase in the form of a white swan.
- C. Jug in the form of a bird's head.
- D. Small flowered white china pot.
- E. Simple white china vase.
    CLOCK
- F. White china pot (as D), surmounted by model aeroplane.
- G. As E.
- H. As C.
- I. White china dog.
- J. As A.
- K. Large snail's shell.

Below Mantelpiece, above Fire
Photograph of boy, in frame decorated with sea-shells. Hanging from the mantelpiece brackets, two poker workings:

1. Picture of Tudor Street seen behind stone steps, with the following verse:

> As we climb the steps of the coming days
> May Health and Friendship Cheer our ways.

2. Done on cardboard, above a floral decoration:

> If we have the Good
> Fortune to win
> A FRIEND
> let us do all rather
> than lose him
> We must Give and Forgive
> Live and let live. We must
> Hope all things. Endure all
> things rather than lose that
> most precious of all
> Earthly Possessions
> a Trusty Friend.
>   *C. Kinglsey*

Plant in a pot in the recess beside the kitchener.
Brassy tin fender in front of the kitchener. Poker.

Hanging on the Dresser shelves
Eight Coronation mugs.
One aluminium jug.
Two large china jugs.
One small mauve china cup.

On the Dresser shelves
Three pairs of small stags' antlers.
Odd rolls of paper.
Snapshot album.

On the Walls
One mirror in a wooden frame.
Fourteen varied pictures, including:.
  One photograph of a brother in the first World War.
  One watercolour of Porlock Weir.
  One flowery garden, with lupins and a thatched cottage.
  One hunting scene (rider with pack of hounds coming towards the onlooker).
  Five photos (sepia) of mountain scenery.
  One peaceful ship scene.
  Two dog pictures.
  One desolate, unframed oil painting of a barren heath and stunted trees.

APPENDIX III
Plan of Luccombe's Geographical Position

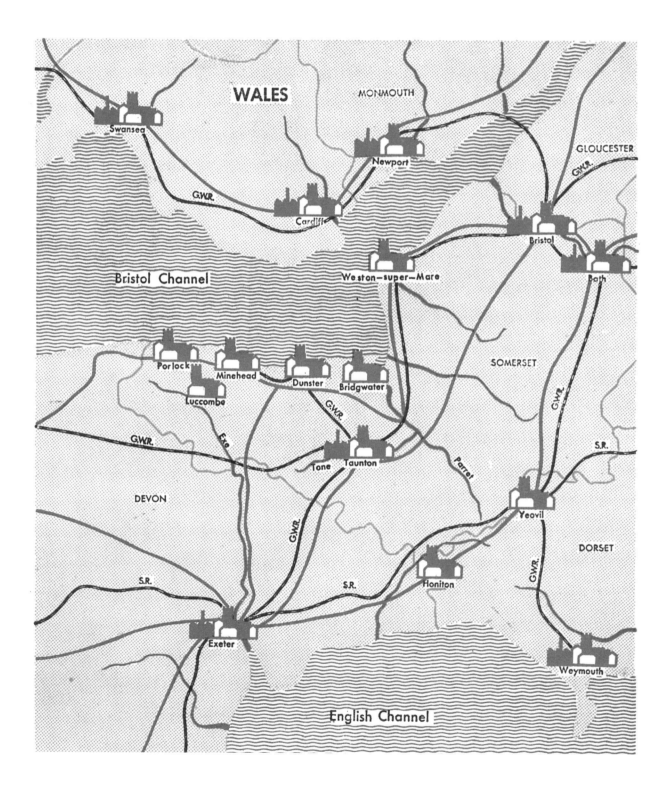

APPENDIX IV
Village Distance Chart

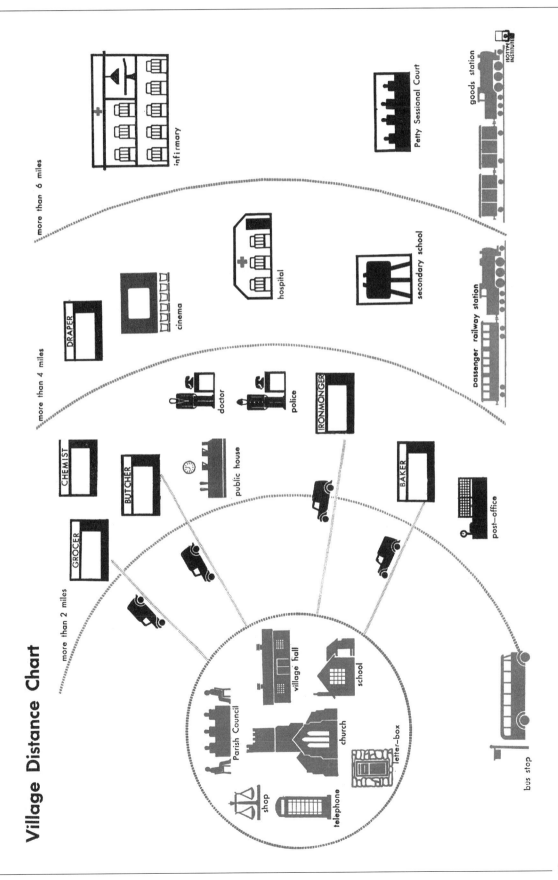

APPENDIX V
Panorama and Plan of Luccombe

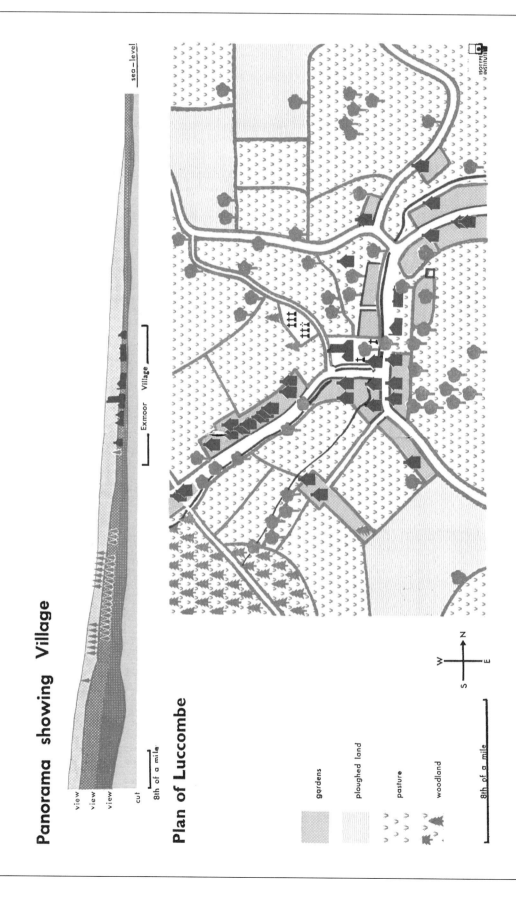

Panorama showing Village

view
view
view
cut

8th of a mile

sea-level

Exmoor Village

Plan of Luccombe

gardens

ploughed land

pasture

woodland

8th of a mile

N
W E
S

APPENDIX VI
A Luccombe Cottage

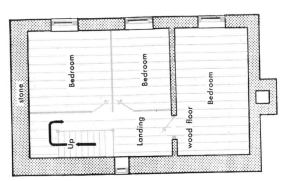

Section of Cottage

Plan of First Floor.

stone
thatch
brick

Bedroom
Bedroom
Bedroom
Landing
wood floor
Up
stone

A Luccombe Cottage

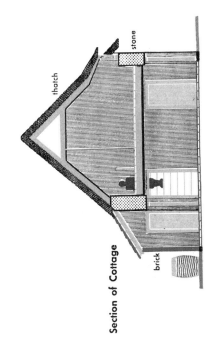

Bird's-eye View of Cottage

Plan of Ground Floor

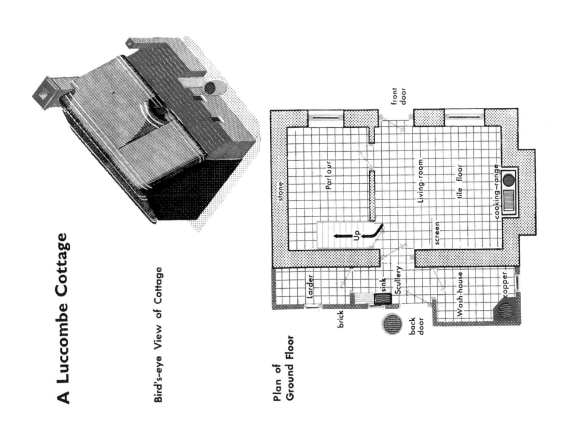

front door
stone
Parlour
Living-room
tile floor
cooking-range
screen
Up
Larder
sink
Scullery
Wash-house
copper
brick
back door

APPENDIX VII
Plan of a Luccombe Cottage Garden